Garland Studies in Historical Demography

Stuart Bruchey

Allan Nevins Professor Emeritus
American Economic History
Columbia University

GENERAL EDITOR

A Garland Series

Garland Studies in
Historical
Demography

Stuart Bruchey

A Garland Series

World Mortality Trends
Since 1870

Jeanne G. Gobalet

GARLAND PUBLISHING, INC.
New York   London
1989

Library of Congress Cataloging-in-Publication Data

Gobalet, Jeanne G.
World mortality trends since 1870 / Jeanne G. Gobalet.
p. cm. — (Garland studies in historical demography)
Based on the author's thesis.
Includes bibliographical references.
ISBN 0-8240-3951-3 (alk. paper)
1. Mortality—History.
I. Title. II. Series.
HB1321.G63 1990
304.6'4'09—dc20   89-29412

Printed on acid-free, 250-year-life paper

Manufactured in the United States of America

TO GARTH

CONTENTS

PREFACE   xv

ACKNOWLEDGMENTS   xvii

Chapter 1   INTRODUCTION   3
             Notes   8

Chapter 2   PREVIOUS THEORY AND RESEARCH: 9
             THE RELATIONSHIPS AMONG
             SOCIOECONOMIC VARIABLES AND
             MORTALITY
             Economic Development   9
             Health Care   11
             Resource Distribution   11
             Summary   14
             Notes   16

Chapter 3   PREVIOUS THEORY AND RESEARCH: 17
             HISTORICAL TRENDS
             Summary   25
             Notes   28

Chapter 4   THEORY AND HYPOTHESES   29
             Introduction   29
             Alternative Theories   31
                Modernization Theory   31
                World System, Dependency Theories   31
                   World System Theory   32
                   Dependency Theory   34
             Time Patterns   37
             Summary   39
             Notes   40

Chapter 5   METHODS AND MEASURES   41
                Panel Analysis   42
                Measures   43
                  Mortality   43
                  Economic Development   45
                  Health Care Availability, Health Aid   45
                  World System Involvement   47
                  Economic Dependence   47
                  Equality   48
                  State Strength   48
                Summary   49
                Notes   52

Chapter 6   RESULTS: LIFE EXPECTANCY TRENDS   53
                Trends   53
                Convergence and Ceilings   58
                Regional Differences   62
                Summary   66
                Notes   67

Chapter 7   RESULTS OF PANEL ANALYSIS   69
                Results   69
                Summary   80
                Notes   81

Chapter 8   RESULTS FROM USE OF NONLINEAR   83
                MODEL
                Nonlinear Model   84
                Results   85
                Combined Effects of Development,
                  Health Care, and Inequality   92
                Summary and Discussion   96

Chapter 9   CONCLUSIONS   101
                Summary of Findings   101
                Research Recommendations   102
                Notes   104

Chapter 10   POLICY IMPLICATIONS   105
             Policies for LDCs   106
             Policies for MDCs   107
             Summary   109
             Notes   110

APPENDIX A: COMPOSITION OF SAMPLES   111

APPENDIX B: LIFE SPAN ESTIMATES FROM THE
NONLINEAR MODEL   123

REFERENCES   129

TABLES

Table

1   Changes Over Time in Factors Affecting Mortality   27

2   Sources of Data   50

3   Effect of Economic Development, Linear Model   70

4   Effect of Health Care, Linear Model   72

5   Effect of International Health Aid, Linear Model   73

6   Effect of World System Involvement, Linear Model   75

7   Effect of Investment Dependence, Linear Model   76

8   Effect of Income Equality, Linear Model   77

9   Effect of State Strength, Linear Model   78

10 Effects of Development, Health Care, and Equality,
    Linear Model   79

11 Effect of Economic Development, Nonlinear Model   86

12 Effect of Health Care, Nonlinear Model   87

13 Effect of International Health Aid, Nonlinear Model   89

14 Effect of World System Involvement, Nonlinear Model   90

15 Effect of Investment Dependence, Nonlinear Model   91

Table

16   Effect of Income Equality, Nonlinear Model   93

17   Effect of State Strength, Nonlinear Model   94

18   Effects of Development, Health Care, and Equality,
      Nonlinear Model   95

19   Summary of Findings from Analyses Using the
      Nonlinear Model   97

ILLUSTRATIONS

Figure

1   Conceptual Model of Factors Affecting Population Growth   5

2   Life Expectancy in MDCs and LDCs, 1950-2025   54

3A   Trends in Life Expectancy in MDCs and LDCs Since 1870   56

3B   Trends in Life Expectancy in MDCs and LDCs Since 1930   57

4A   Proportion of MDC Mean Life Expectancy Experienced in LDCs Since 1870   60

4B   Proportion of MDC Mean Life Expectancy Experienced in LDCs Since 1930   61

5A   Regional Trends in Life Expectancy: Western and Latin American Nations   64

5B   Regional Trends in Life Expectancy: Asian and African Nations   65

6   Location of MDCs ("West") Used in Samples   112

7   Location of LDCs Used in Samples   114

8   Location of Latin American Countries Used in Samples   116

9   Location of Asian Countries Used in Samples   118

10   Location of African Countries Used in Samples   120

PREFACE

This work gives a sociological overview of theoretical and empirical work on the history of mortality. It identifies the factors which have produced mortality reduction and describes life expectancy trends in individual countries and geographical regions from 1870 until the late 1980s. It presents a comprehensive examination of the patterns and causes of historical mortality trends.

Theoretical explanations for mortality differentials are reviewed in Chapters 2, 3 and 4 and serve as the basis for a series of hypotheses which are tested statistically. Graphs presented in Chapter 6 illustrate the dramatic differences in mortality trends in more- and less-developed countries. They disclose that since 1960 the rate of convergence of mortality levels has slowed. In the 1970s and 1980s, less developed countries gave signs of approaching maximum life expectancies much lower than those of the more-developed countries.

Factors which affect life expectancy levels and trends include economic development, availability of health care, international health aid, income distribution, dependence on foreign investment, state (government) strength, and world system involvement. Models of the effects of these variables on life expectancy during various time periods are estimated using panel analysis, described in Chapter 5. Results are described in Chapters 7, 8 and 9. These results reveal scant evidence of recent shifts in the relative importance of variables and tend to refute assertions made by theorists in the 1970s and early 1980s.

This monograph revises a doctoral dissertation in Sociology completed in 1982 at Stanford University: *Causes of World Mortality Decline, 1870-1980*. The graphs have been updated to include data through 1987. References to research and theoretical literature have been updated to reflect material published through mid-1989. The regression analyses reported in Chapters 7 and 8 were not updated, but to do so will be worthwhile when life expectancy data for 1990 become available.

Since work on this investigation began, mortality research has begun to come into its own. There have been increasing case studies, historical investigations, and especially discussions of health and mortality policy (see Chapter 10). Mortality probably is still less-studied than fertility and migration, but many demographers, sociologists, economists, and other social scientists are giving attention to the topic. It unquestionably merits such emphasis.

ACKNOWLEDGMENTS

This book would not have been possible without help. My father, Kenneth C. Gobalet, spent many hours drawing graphs, proofreading, and preparing figures and tables, some at the very last minute. My son, Robert Gallatin Gobalet Norton, aged five, cooperated (most of the time). My husband, Garth L. Norton, to whom this work is dedicated, helped Rob cooperate and provided endless encouragement. I thank each for assisting me as he did.

The doctoral dissertation upon which this monograph is based was completed with the guidance of Professors Dudley Kirk, John W. Meyer and Michael T. Hannan. Their contributions are appreciated. Other Stanford University faculty, staff, and graduate students were supportive. The Stanford Sociology Department, Food Research Institute, and Center for information Technology assisted in various ways. The people of the San Jose Community College District, the State of California, and the United States deserve thanks for subsidizing my work through payment of taxes.

WORLD MORTALITY TRENDS SINCE 1870

Chapter 1

INTRODUCTION

Since longevity is an ultimate measure of human welfare, one of the greatest achievements of western civilization is the recent dramatic reduction of mortality. In the last two centuries citizens of developed countries have gained an average of more than 30 years of life. More recently, people in non-western, poorer countries have also benefited. From 1900 to the present, life expectancies at birth more than doubled in the less developed countries.[1] These gains in life expectancy are usually attributed to economic development and to the worldwide diffusion of great advances in public health. Both development and diffusion are to some extent a product of a country's assimilation into the modern world. This study investigates the effects of social and economic factors on mortality. Particular attention is paid to the effects of diffusion of ideas and the distribution of various resources within societies and worldwide.

Social scientists have long concerned themselves with explaining the causes and consequences of social stratification. However, much of stratification theory focuses on analyzing the reasons for and patterns of resource distribution within and across societies, rather than on clarifying the outcomes of the distribution with respect to human welfare, including human life itself. Weber (1946) defined a class in terms of its life chances, which result from the distribution of economic resources and opportunities. Certainly life chances include chances for life, or life expectancy, and mortality relates to economic circumstances of the class. Variations in mortality reflect variations in the real welfare of groups. Mortality varies over time, internationally, and intranationally. These variations result from inequalities in the distribution of economic resources and opportunities.

This investigation focuses on one aspect of the demographic transition, an ongoing worldwide change in vital rates and population growth patterns which began in Europe before 1800. The transition has included declines in vital rates, usually beginning with mortality reduction; though in some European populations fertility reduction may have begun earlier. Mortality reduction resulted in rapid population growth followed, in some countries, by fertility declines and slower population growth. In both more developed countries (MDCs) and less developed countries (LDCs), there has been considerable temporal variation between the onset of mortality decline and that of fertility reduction.

Though certainly as many different demographic transitions take place as there are societies, it is nevertheless often assumed that there are underlying similarities in transition patterns. Implicit in most discussions of the demographic transition is the conceptual model illustrated in Figure 1.[2] In this model the natural environment loosely constrains potential variation in economic and social patterns. Economic and social factors include economic development, standard of living, income, and income distribution. Others are religion and the availability of health care, education, government old age security programs, and family planning programs. Still other economic and social factors are the country's level of modernization and incorporation into the world system.[3] Some of these are internal structural characteristics of the society. Some are influenced by forces external to the society. Motivations, attitudes, and values include expectations about future income, upward mobility, and cost of children. Also included are dependence of the aged on children for support and for carrying on the family name. Other attitudes are confidence in science and technology and feelings of personal efficacy and control over one's own destiny. Values include beliefs about the ideal age for marriage, ideal family size, desirability of large families, and sex roles within marriage. According to Davis and Blake (1956), intermediate variables include factors affecting exposure to intercourse, conception, gestation, and parturition.

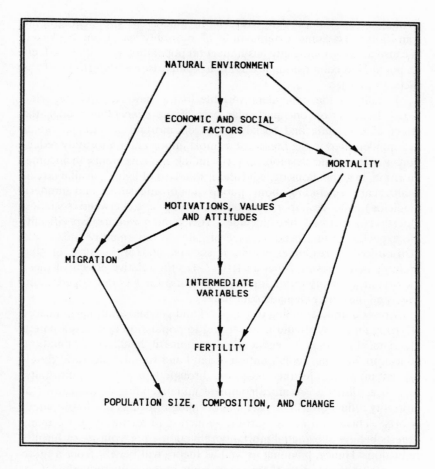

Figure 1. Conceptual Model of Factors Affecting Population Growth

This model or a similar one is used in demographic transition theory. Though the object of that theory is to explain changes in population size and composition, much research on the demographic transition focuses only on the causes of fertility changes. Because the values, attitudes, and motivations affecting the intermediate variables are influenced by the prevailing mortality characteristics of the social group (especially infant and child mortality), mortality has usually been treated as an independent variable in studies of the demographic transition. To some extent study of mortality has been neglected because although mortality has impact on population growth, its effects on population composition are small in comparison with fertility effects (Schoen 1986).

Mortality is the dependent variable in the new research reported here. Focus is on one particular part of the conceptual model, the effect of economic and social factors on mortality. The particular factors identified in the literature as most important in mortality reduction are economic development (including improvements in income, nutrition, hygiene, housing, education, standard of living), availability of health care (including both public health measures and modern medicine), and resource distribution within and between societies. Questions addressed here include: Has human welfare (specifically, life expectancy) improved because of gains in the quantity and/or the distribution of resources within a society, and/or because of that society's contacts with other societies? Do the relative effects of these factors on mortality differ for developed and for less developed countries, and have they changed over time?

Increased understanding of temporal and spatial variations in factors affecting mortality should prove useful to population and development planners. Programs for economic development, health and sanitation, education, housing, redistribution of land and wealth, and rural development may affect fertility indirectly, through their effects on mortality, as well as directly. A more complete understanding of the causes of mortality reduction will be useful in deciding priorities for development efforts. This could hasten fertility reduction in a country, since many experts believe substantial mortality reduction a prerequisite of fertility reduction. Hence, planning as well as theory will benefit from a more complete understanding of the antecedents of mortality reduction.

In addition to attempting to answer the substantive questions posed above, this work advances new methodologies. Mortality research has heretofore suffered from haphazard, ineffective modeling and data analysis. One reason for these weaknesses is lack of theoretical grounding for research. Another is the tendency to explain variance and to perform oversimplified cross-sectional analyses when the real objective is to study change over time. Theoretical formulations are presented in Chapter 4. Panel analysis and a nonlinear model were used to estimate effects on mortality of economic development, health measures, and other factors. The results appear in Chapters 7 and 8 and Chapter 9 contains a discussion of the findings. Policy implications of mortality trends are discussed in Chapter 10.

Notes

1. Less developed countries (LDCs) include those of Latin America and the Caribbean, Africa, the Middle East, Asia (except Japan and the Soviet Union), and Oceania (except Australia and New Zealand). More developed countries (MDCs) include the United States, Canada, the nations of Europe, and the exceptions noted above. To be consistent, this division is used throughout. See Appendix A for maps and lists of the LDCs and MDCs studied. Preston (1980) estimated 1900 life expectancy at birth to be about 27.5 years in LDCs, and in the late 1980s it was about 60 years (compared with about 75 years in MDCs).

2. The figure is simplified for purposes of clarity: some arrows have been omitted. For example, as Scrimshaw (1978) asserted, fertility level may affect infant and child mortality.

3. The term "world system" is used by some social scientists to emphasize the interrelationships among societies, political systems, and economies. World system theory, discussed in Chapter 4, emphasizes the impact of dominant ("core") societies on subordinate ("peripheral") societies. Incorporation into the world system occurs as peripheral societies come under the influence of core societies through the processes of colonization, cultural diffusion, and economic exchange.

Chapter 2

PREVIOUS THEORY AND RESEARCH:
THE RELATIONSHIPS AMONG SOCIOECONOMIC
VARIABLES AND MORTALITY

Various sociologists, demographers, and economists have investigated relationships among economic development, availability of health care, resource distribution, and mortality within and across societies. Explanations for the relationships have usually been *a priori*, pragmatic, and atheoretical. Most analytical work has been cross-sectional, and none of the studies has examined the simultaneous effects of all three socioeconomic variables on mortality.[1] Nevertheless, both descriptive and analytical efforts suggest that each of these variables does affect mortality and that they are interrelated as well; though differences of opinion exist about their comparative importance.

A. ECONOMIC DEVELOPMENT

Hauser (1959) and Stockwell (1960) investigated the feasibility of using demographic measures to indicate economic development level indirectly. They found rather high correlations between demographic and economic indicators. However, this association may be explained

9

by economic development leading to reduced mortality, especially when development brings improved health services and education. It is also likely that diffusion of nutrition, health, technology, and investments from other societies triggers economic development and/or lower mortality, especially in less developed countries (LDCs) in recent decades. Hauser's and Stockwell's ideas have value, but economic data today are considered at least as valid as demographic data, so vital rates are not usually substituted for economic measures in research.

An investigation of the relationship between economic development and vital rates by Oechsli and Kirk (1975) found an inverse relationship between per capita gross national product and crude death rate. In a cross-sectional analysis of Latin American and Caribbean nations mortality and fertility declines were viewed as part of the multifaceted, but holistic, process of development. These declines were regarded as sensitive indicators of level of economic development. Oechsli and Kirk found mortality declines early in the development process in Latin America, and fertility declines later, after an economic threshold (of about $500-1000 per capita gross national product, as of the 1960s) was reached. They felt expectation of life at birth superior to crude death rates as an indicator of modernization, because life expectancy is not affected by the age structure of the population and because life expectancy is increasing faster in LDCs than in more developed countries (MDCs). They found that decline in mortality (or increase in life expectancy) has a clear relationship to economic development and fertility decline, though they assume income distribution within societies may affect the relationship.

Sagan and Afifi (1978) concluded from their cross-sectional correlation and regression analyses of life expectancy and infant mortality that literacy and per capita energy consumption were the two most important specific factors in reducing mortality since 1900. Even more important in mortality trends was a "time factor" which has added 18 years to life expectancy, independent of economic development, since 1900. They asserted that this time effect might reflect a change in the virulence of infectious agents and/or in an improvement in human resistance to disease. Perhaps a more likely explanation is that their methodology was inadequate to test respective influences of the relevant health, development, and distribution factors.

B. HEALTH CARE

Palloni (1985) studied mortality change in Latin America since the 1950s and found that in some countries, mortality decline was not sustained because efforts were almost exclusively devoted to "vertical interventions." These are vector eradication programs like anti-malaria campaigns, vaccination programs, provision of sulfonamides and antibiotics, and rehydration treatment against diarrhea. More sustained mortality reduction was achieved in those countries which experienced socioeconomic development and used "nonvertical interventions," providing widespread access to medical services, improving water supplies and sanitation, and supporting nutritional campaigns and family health programs.

Adelman (1963) conducted a cross-sectional analysis of vital rates and development indicators and found that industrialization has a significant effect on life expectancy. She suggested that after initial mortality reduction is achieved through public health and sanitation measures, internal economic growth may be required for further reduction. Increases in per capita income, education, urbanization, and distribution of health and welfare services may be needed for LDCs to sustain mortality declines.

Schultz (1976) suggested that public health measures may reduce infant and child mortality from some causes, but that high levels of diarrheal disease and mortality can be reduced only through increased education (especially of women), increased personal income, and more equal income distribution. These result in better nutrition and living conditions. He stated that differences in age patterns of mortality between MDCs and LDCs are explained by household-level sanitation.

C. RESOURCE DISTRIBUTION

Stockwell (1962) and Antonovsky (1967) investigated the relationship between mortality and socioeconomic status. Stockwell suggested that mortality (especially infant mortality) might be used to compare levels of social and economic well-being across societies, especially between modern urban-industrial societies and the LDCs. In a review of studies of mortality and social class in MDCs, Antonovsky found significant class mortality differentials, especially between the lowest class and other social strata, and for the middle-aged. Sometimes the class differences were greater for women than for men, probably because women have made greater gains in life expectancy. Though class mortality differences were reduced in the twentieth century, recently the closing of the gap has slowed or halted. Antonovsky hypothesized that when mortality rates are either very high or very low, class mortality differences tend to be small. When class differences are small, mortality does not change significantly. When they are large, many deaths should be preventable. Most LDCs have infant mortality levels and life expectancies which could be significantly altered though application of existing health, nutrition, and sanitation knowledge, and through social welfare programs designed to distribute these more equitably. Antonovsky implied that economic development and greater equality would lower mortality and increase life expectancy in LDCs. Preston (1978b) asserted that within both MDCs and LDCs, mortality variations are closely related to socioeconomic status. Mortality differentials (and overall mortality levels) could be reduced by narrowing socioeconomic differences among groups by resource redistribution as well as by overall economic development.

Adelman and Morris (1973) studied the relationship between income distribution and economic development. Their results suggest that after public health measures have been introduced from outside the country, further significant mortality reductions are unlikely until additional economic growth occurs, with government participation in development and resource distribution or redistribution. The diffusion of health technology from MDCs to LDCs may therefore increase mortality differences within the LDCs, though it reduces mortality in the society as a whole.

Johansson and Mosk (1987) studied Japan's mortality transition and found that because the Japanese government was willing to import and distribute public health technologies after the Meiji restoration (1868), by 1900 "underdeveloped" Japan achieved a life expectancy at birth comparable to that of Great Britain and Italy. Between 1900 and World War II, the Japanese government emphasized military expenditure, de-emphasizing public health, and Japan's life expectancy remained at the level of 1900 until after the war. In the postwar years,

Japan's remarkable improvement in life expectancy was achieved through disease control (including use of antibiotics and vaccines), increased public health spending, and urbanization (with availability of high quality health care and public health measures to urban populations). By 1960 Japanese male life expectancy at birth was greater than that of American males, though Japan's per capita income was less than one-third that of the U.S. Japan exemplifies a country which has devoted public resources to health-improving measures and thereby achieved, through redistribution, high life expectancies (by the late 1980s, the highest in the world).

Ahluwalia (1974, 1976) studied the relationships between income inequality and economic development in a cross-section of MDCs and LDCs. He found, as Kuznets (1955 and 1980) and others including Lenski (1966) had predicted, that a nonmonotonic, inverted-U-shaped relationship exists between inequality and development level in all nations, such that income inequality increases during the earlier stages of economic development, and declines thereafter. Later in the development process, a more equitable distribution of income may result from shifts in the structure of productivity, expansion of education, increasing skill in the labor force, and reduction in population growth rate. Presumably, increased equality of income distribution leads to mortality reduction.

Participants in the 1979 United Nations/World Health Organization meeting in Mexico City (Meeting on the Socioeconomic Determinants and Consequences of Mortality) concluded that for the previous 25 years, mortality differentials and socioeconomic gaps had persisted in the MDCs, despite consistent mortality decline. In France and the United Kingdom there may even have been an increase in social class differences in mortality (U.N. and W.H.O. 1979 and 1981).

Little research focuses on the combined effects of development and distribution of resources on mortality. Preston (1978b) compared the experiences of Sri Lanka, Kerala (state in India), and Cuba with those of Bahrain, Iraq, Saudi Arabia, and the Yemen Arab Republic. The former group of states made special efforts to increase literacy, spread public health measures, and improve nutrition (the last in Sri Lanka and Cuba but not in Kerala), and achieved mortality reduction far beyond that of states with comparable per capita gross national products. The latter group of states achieved marked increases in national income from 1970-1975, but had relatively modest mortality reduction. Preston concluded that unstructured development cannot produce anything resembling the significant mortality reduction resulting from deliberate programs to distribute resources equitably.

In a cross-sectional study of 56 countries, Rodgers (1979) attempted to explain differences in life expectancy (at ages 0 and 5) and infant mortality in terms of per capita income and its distribution. He found a robust negative partial correlation between inequality in personal income and life expectancy, holding constant the nonlinear effect of national per capita income level. It was assumed that the higher the income level, the smaller the effect of increased income on life expectancy. Greater inequality was always associated with higher mortality. The difference between a relatively egalitarian country and a relatively inegalitarian country in life expectancy at birth is likely to be as much as five to ten years.

Preston (1980) compared the relative effects of national per capita income and income distribution on life expectancy in a sample of 52 countries as of about 1970. He concluded that the relations between mortality and income at the national level are dominated by the relations between mortality and individual income (income distribution). However, Parks (1980) suggested that because Preston's measure of income distribution did not correct for the age distribution of the population, the results of his analysis were biased and that the effect of national income on life expectancy actually is important. Questions about the size and nature of effects of economic development and distribution of material and nonmaterial resources on mortality remain.

D. SUMMARY

The descriptive and analytical work discussed above lead to three assertions:

1. The process of economic development reduces mortality, though there may be temporal variations in the relationship between economic development and mortality.

2.   Health care availability reduces mortality.

3.   Equality of resource distribution reduces mortality, so that countries with similar per capita income levels can have different mortality patterns.

Various investigators have examined the impact of relations among countries in the modern world system. The next chapter reviews the literature on changes over time in the relative importance of development, health care, equality, and other factors on mortality in MDCs and LDCs and the consequences (for mortality) of position in the world system.

Notes

1. Numerous studies have been conducted exploring changing patterns
   of morbidity and causes of death, such as diseases, accidents, and so
   forth (Preston and Nelson 1974; Preston 1976, 1978b, 1980;
   Bourgeois-Pichat 1985). These excellent analyses are not reviewed
   here, since focus is on the socioeconomic variables influencing mortality rather than on the diseases which cause death. It is nevertheless interesting to note that Bourgeois-Pichat (1985) states that since
   1965 the variance of life expectancy in MDCs has increased because
   of changing patterns in cause of death. While Japan's life expectancy has risen, the U.S.S.R.'s has fallen. Eastern European life expectancy has stagnated or declined slightly. Bourgeois-Pichat states
   this increased spread of mortality in MDCs is caused mostly by
   divergence in cardiovascular disease mortality. Japan and some
   other countries have reduced such deaths, while Eastern European
   countries Bourgeois-Pichat calls "laggard" have experienced
   increases.

Chapter 3

PREVIOUS THEORY AND RESEARCH:
HISTORICAL TRENDS

Discussions of the demographic transition often assert or imply that mortality reduction results from economic development and contributes to fertility reduction after a certain development level or threshold is reached (Rich 1973; King 1974; Oechsli and Kirk 1975; Simon 1976; Singer 1976; U.N. 1980). Some have intimated that there are similar thresholds in patterns of factors affecting mortality change: hypothetical points which mark changes in the relative influence of factors endogenous and exogenous to a society and/or changes in the relative importance of development, health inputs, and resource distribution. Until requisite levels of these factors are achieved, the speed of mortality improvement might slow or mortality rates might remain constant.

Omran developed a description of historical mortality change which he called "epidemiologic transition theory" (1971 and 1983). The transition involved a shift in the leading causes of death from pandemics to degenerative and man-made diseases. Pandemic diseases began to retreat in Europe, influenced by ecobiologic and socioeconomic factors, by the late eighteenth century. In LDCs this occurred in the twentieth century, speeded by importation of medical technology and public health measures. Countries experienced diverse patterns of mortality reduction.[1] Omran concluded that further socio-economic development, public health inputs, and improved resource

17

distribution are essential to added mortality reduction in LDCs.

In the 1950s, researchers suggested that there had been changes in variables affecting mortality (Davis 1956; Stolnitz 1955 and 1956), implying the existence of thresholds. They proposed that until relatively recently, levels of and variations in mortality were determined mostly by factors within a society, such as standard of living, environmental conditions, and distribution of resources. More recently, mortality has been increasingly influenced by factors external to a society, especially the diffusion of health technologies and medicines from more developed nations (Davis 1956; U.N. 1953 and 1973).

Even in the MDCs, public health, sanitation and medicine did not become important factors in mortality reduction until after the mid-1800s. Before that time, decreases in mortality resulted mostly from improvements in living standards (Schultz 1976; Arriaga and Davis 1969), caused by various factors, including changing immunological patterns (Schofield 1984) and increased food supplies available in Europe after about 1700 (McKeown 1976). Except for smallpox inoculation, public health and other medical improvements had little impact. Mortality was mostly a function of environmental factors, including endemic and epidemic disease patterns. Mortality tended to be higher in cities than in rural areas. The rate of mortality improvement was lowest in countries with the highest mortality levels and lowest economic position (Arriaga and Davis, 1969). If anything, mortality differences *increased* across societies, with northwest European nations (especially rural regions) having substantially lower mortality than eastern Europe and the Balkans (Kunitz 1983). Kunitz (1986) asserted that as a result of the evolution of stable nation states, by the late eighteenth century northwest European countries were increasingly able to begin to control epidemic infectious diseases. They could control their armies, borders, and internal affairs and they therefore could encourage industry, develop transportation, and occasionally redistribute resources and diminish the impact of smallpox, malaria, and plague.

After about 1880, discovery and diffusion of scientific knowledge and public health technology became increasingly important in MDCs. Acceptance of the germ theory of disease resulted in more widespread environmental sanitation and development of methods to control infectious diseases, especially endemic infectious diseases like tuberculosis and diarrheas (Kunitz 1986). According to McKeown

(1976), exposure to infection was reduced mainly by improving hygiene concerning water and food. The improvement of water supplies and sewage disposal in the second half of the nineteenth century was especially important. Such measures originated in the most developed societies of northwestern Europe and reduced overall mortality and class differences in mortality. During the late 1800s and early 1900s, mortality reduction techniques spread to North America, Eastern and Southern Europe, and to European populations elsewhere, including Australia and New Zealand (Arriaga and Davis 1969).

By about 1930, some less developed areas began to benefit from diffused knowledge so that rapid mortality reduction occurred independent of further economic development (Adelman 1963; Arriaga 1970a and b; Arriaga and Davis 1969; Davis 1956; Preston 1976 and 1978b; Schultz 1976; Stolnitz 1965; Kunitz 1986). Relatively minor investments in public health programs and international health aid resulted in unprecedented mortality declines in Latin America, Asia, and eventually in Africa (Davis 1956).[2] These measures were introduced earliest in Japan, then in other areas in contact with MDCs, particularly the most European parts of Latin America (southern and urban), and somewhat later, in the areas of Asia most influenced by Europe. Sri Lanka, for example, benefited from better water supplies and sewage disposal systems in the early 1900s (U.N. 1986a). The regions to receive the advances last, and therefore to experience mortality reduction latest, were in Africa and the non-European parts of Latin America and Asia.

By the 1930s, modern medicine and scientific technology began to have significant mortality-reducing effects in MDCs. Biomedical (especially pharmaceutical) and chemical advances produced the sulfonamides, antimicrobial drugs, and insecticides such as DDT (Preston 1978b; McDermott 1980). Most of these were developed between 1931 and 1951 (McDermott 1980). As a result, age-specific death rates fell suddenly and sharply in the United States and other MDCs. By the 1960s these measures also had substantial mortality-lessening impact in the LDCs, helping reduce levels of some endemic infectious diseases. By the mid-twentieth century non-infectious diseases like cardiovascular diseases and cancer became the leading causes of death in MDCs.

Beginning about 1960, new ceilings of mortality reduction were reached and new shifts in patterns of factors influencing deaths occurred. Adelman (1963) and Schultz (1976) suggested that when the diffusion of health technology and medicine reaches a threshold, resource distribution once again becomes more important in mortality reduction. They implied that in recent decades mortality in LDCs is increasingly associated with development and distribution, and decreasingly associated with additional public health improvements (except insofar as development results in introduction of advanced health technologies.)

Grosse and Perry (1982) performed various correlation analyses of life expectancy, health expenditures, health facilities and personnel, sanitation activities and water supplies, social indicators, and economic indicators in LDCs in the 1960s and 1970s. They concluded that whereas economic indicators had the strongest association with life expectancy in the 1960s, social variables (literacy) had the strongest association in the 1970s. Grosse and Perry's methodology provides only tentative indication of changing temporal patterns in factors related to life expectancy. Correlation analysis is a rather weak (and often misleading) method for analyzing causational change.[3]

Behm (1979) found great heterogeneity of mortality in different populations within Latin American countries. Around 1970, lower socioeconomic groups had risks of dying four to five times higher than more affluent groups in the same society. Behm felt that these inequalities are similar to those which existed in Europe a century ago. He advocated a more equitable distribution of medical resources and income.

Kunitz (1986) stated that endemic infectious diseases persist in regions where social inequality is great and agricultural wage laborers are exploited, particularly in Latin America. He noted that economic development has the potential to eliminate endemic infectious diseases as a significant cause of death. He pointed out (as did Thomas Malthus nearly two centuries ago) that mortality conditions vary greatly within and across societies, and whether mortality improvement occurs depends on the actions of members of each society.

Infant and child mortality remain rather high in many LDCs, especially in Subsaharan Africa. Further improvements there will depend on economic progress leading to better nutrition, adequate sewage disposal systems, pure water supplies, effective transportation networks, more and better health facilities and more and better-trained health personnel (U.N. 1979). Gaisie (1981) stated that in the 1950s the pace of mortality decline slowed in tropical Africa because the potential of public health measures (introduced by colonial regimes and through international health assistance) was exhausted. Until economic and social developments result in improved living standards, further reduction in mortality will be difficult to achieve. Until inequalities in health care are reduced, mortality will remain high. According to Azefor (1981) even Subsaharan urban areas have high mortality (sometimes higher than rural areas) because rapid urban growth has resulted in overcrowding and miserable living standards for the urban poor.

Preston (1978b) felt that beginning in the late 1960s, development might again be assuming a dominant role in mortality trends in LDCs because health interventions had reached a state of diminishing returns, or a ceiling. Causes of death patterns in LDCs showed increasing prevalence of poverty-related diseases and decreasing occurrence of diseases easily reduced through specific health measures. He also noted that the United States, the largest contributor to international health programs, had a diminishing commitment to those programs. He recommended testing the proposition that development factors (rather than health-promoting inputs) have assumed a dominant role in LDCs' mortality trends since the 1960s. (By "development factors," he probably meant resource distribution.)

In a more recent study, Preston (1986) found that for the decade beginning 1965-69, income, literacy, and nutrition were the dominant factors in explaining mortality decline. During that period, exogenous factors (like antimalarial programs, immunization and other vertical governmental and international programs, and improvements in personal health practices) operated with sharply reduced intensity. Decreased commitment to international health assistance on the part of some MDCs may have contributed. Preston was able, however, to include in his analyses only measures of life expectancy at birth, infant mortality, per capita income (gross domestic product per capita and International Comparison Project figures for purchasing power), literacy, and per capita calorie consumption. He did not perform analyses of the impact of any "exogenous" variables on mortality.

Rogers and Wofford (1989) studied 95 LDCs. They concluded that in the 1970s and 1980s life expectancy was affected primarily by socioeconomic development and secondarily by public health measures. Their research methods were relatively simple and analyses were

affected by problems of multicollinearity.   Also, they apparently
neglected to control for 1975 level of life expectancy in analyzing the
effects of various development and health measures in 1975 (or
thereabouts) on 1985 life expectancy.

The pace of mortality reduction was decelerating in the 1960s and
1970s in both MDCs and LDCs, approaching asymptotes (Arriaga
1981; Gwatkin 1980; Palloni 1981a and b; U.N. 1979 and 1982). The
reasons for decreasing rates of improvement differed in MDCs and
LDCs. In MDCs, most of the capabilities of medical knowledge and
technology have been realized: infectious diseases are rarely fatal
there. Mortality in the first 50 years of life is very low even though few
new antimicrobial drugs have been developed in the last several
decades (McDermott 1980). Degenerative diseases affecting older
people have only recently begun to be reduced (U.N. 1980; Crimmins
1981), and there is a potential for substantial reduction. By the early
1980s, Japan passed Sweden to become the country with the longest life
expectancy at birth, largely because of reduction of mortality from
diseases of the circulatory system in those aged 55 and over
(Yanagishita and Guralnik 1988).

In some of the LDCs, especially in Latin America and Asia, mortality reduction decelerated because borrowed medical technology
achieved most of its potential for health improvement through
immunization and control of contagious disease. Accinelli and Mueller
(1980) asserted that mortality levels in MDCs and LDCs will not
converge because of great disparity in economic development and the
high cost of additional improvements in living standards in LDCs.
Using Argentina as an example (where life expectancy decreased
slightly between 1960 and 1970), they concluded that there is a
threshold leading to lower mortality rates a country can cross only in
conjunction with a substantial rise in economic development and living
standards. Arriaga (1981) likewise stated that further mortality reduction in Latin America requires improvement in living standards of the
lowest socioeconomic groups.

Palloni (1981a and b) concluded that Latin America's slowed mortality decline and excessive infant and child mortality can be explained
in terms of regional differences in the demographic transition.   In
Western Europe and North America, economic development and,
later, medical advances (chiefly public health measures) reduced death
rates. In Latin America, death rates dropped because of public health

measures, but lack of subsequent economic development caused these rates to stabilize at levels higher than was the pattern in Europe. These higher levels might be temporary: Palloni's cross-sectional analysis led him to conclude that improvements in education (which he considered a development measure) will eventually contribute to further mortality reduction.

Ruzicka and Hansluwka (1982) found that in the 1950s and 1960s health care and improved living standards reduced mortality in low income countries in south and east Asia. In the 1970s the pace of mortality reduction slowed. The slowing of mortality decline occurred at relatively high levels of mortality. Differences in mortality levels between subgroups of national populations remained large, and the slowing of mortality reduction paralleled slowing economic growth. Economic change produced larger proportions of groups at risk of higher mortality within populations.

In empirical studies of these recent trends, Preston compared cross-sectional mortality patterns about 1930 and 1960 (1976) and about 1940 and 1970 (1980). He concluded that during these periods life expectancy gains for the world as a whole resulted not from increases in national per capita incomes, literacy, or improved nutrition, but from factors external to a country's level of per capita income. Most important among these was the diffusion of medical and public health technology from MDCs to LDCs. He also found a shift from the earlier period to the later one in the causes of death for populations at equivalent mortality levels. He believes that diffusion of health technology plus an overall acceleration of demographic changes account for this shift.

The United Nations (1988) reported that the annual rate of life expectancy improvement accelerated in Africa from the 1950s to the 1980s.[4] Asian life expectancy improved more rapidly in the 1960s to 1970s, and more slowly before and after. The MDCs' and Latin America's rates of improvement dropped dramatically in the 1960s to 1980s (though improvement remained the pattern). When the level of life expectancy at the start of the period was considered, those countries with the lowest initial levels of life expectancy sustained the highest (and increasing) rates of improvement.

Sell and Kunitz (1986-7) concluded that slowing rates of Asian and Latin American LDC mortality decline during the 1970s and 1980s resulted partly from growing indebtedness of those LDCs. The economic conditions present in those countries introduced new kinds of health hazards at the same time public health progress was declining. New health hazards included those associated with urbanization, increased tobacco consumption, unsafe occupational practices, and unhealthy diets.

Mosk and Johannson (1986) described the mortality transition in MDCs as a four-stage process. They stated that whereas initially per capita income and mortality were uncorrelated, the process of development led first to a strong positive correlation, then a weaker positive correlation, then a negative correlation, and finally a weaker negative correlation. The first transitional stage occurred when economic development began in parts of Europe, and there came to be a positive relationship between income and mortality. This was because there was minimal public health technology and regions with higher per capita income tended to have larger cities and more hazardous working conditions than those with lower income. The second stage existed in Western Europe when, by the late nineteenth century, limited public health advances reduced the strength of the positive correlation between mortality and income. The more developed regions began to have improved urban living conditions and education for more citizens (particularly girls), which resulted in slightly lower mortality levels. Third, about 1910 European per capita income and mortality began to be negatively related so that wealthier regions and socioeconomic groups enjoyed longer lives. Public health measures were exported by MDCs during this period. Fourth, by the 1960s low income areas of MDCs experienced improved living conditions. Public health measures and modern medicine spread so that most members of society benefited and income and mortality once again became less negatively correlated. Intranational differences (class-related) in mortality varied from one MDC to another. In some more developed regions (e.g., Scandinavia) class differentials in mortality were substantially reduced. In others, these differentials persisted (e.g., Great Britain and the United States). Only a few LDCs (Kerala state, Sri Lanka, Costa Rica, and China) committed resources to health improvement to reach this fourth stage, in which mortality is low. These LDCs do not resemble the MDCs in income levels, but have the same negative correlation between income and mortality.

Increasingly, it is suggested, individuals' choices of life style are influencing mortality within MDCs and to a lesser extent in LDCs

(Vallin 1981; Nightingale 1981; Antonovsky 1981; U.N. 1984, 1985, and 1988; Rogers and Hackenberg 1987). Some of the life styles which are associated with higher or lower rates of morbidity and mortality are class-related. These life styles are evidenced by smoking, excessive alcohol consumption, unhealthy dietary practices, lack of exercise, homosexuality, sexual promiscuity, intravenous drug use, accidents, suicide, homicide, and decision to vaccinate children. It is suggested that education and more responsible individual behavior can reduce preventable or premature deaths from these causes.

SUMMARY

The literature presents a bewildering assortment of information, research and interpretation regarding the causes of mortality decline during the last century. It is clear that mortality dropped faster during some periods than others and more rapidly in LDCs than in MDCs. Recently the rate of mortality decline has slowed in some regions. The causes of decline have differed in MDCs and LDCs, and the relative contributions of various causes have shifted over time.

The factors most often mentioned in the literature as influencing the process of mortality reduction are economic development, public health measures and medical technology, and distribution of resources. Shifts in relative importance of these factors are assumed to have occurred at approximately 1880, 1930, and 1960. The explanation most often given for these shifts is a "threshold," "ceiling," or "diminishing returns" effect. At each threshold, the relative importance of factors affecting mortality are assumed to have changed.

A summary of the supposed shifting patterns of factors causing mortality reduction in MDCs and LDCs is presented in Table 1. Countries reach thresholds at different times because of their varied socioeconomic histories. Those countries which are today more developed experienced simultaneous economic and technological advances. Their first threshold occurred when public health technology became sufficiently sophisticated to reduce mortality. Benefits of many types of modernization extended widely throughout populations. Later, a new threshold was crossed when medical and pharmaceutical technology began to be most influential in further mortality reduction. Still more recently, the effects of medicine reached a ceiling so that distribution of economic resources within MDCs and the life styles chosen by individuals have the greatest impact on aggregate mortality levels.

LDCs experienced introduction of public health measures from outside without the broad-spectrum socioeconomic modernization experience by MDCs. Inexpensive health technology which had been developed in MDCs reduced mortality rapidly, especially infant mortality. Recently, LDCs experienced a saturation of cheap medical technology, so that further economic development and redistribution of resources will be required for additional mortality decline.

Reasons for the noted shifts and different patterns of mortality reduction in MDCs and LDCs are usually not discussed in detail in the literature. There has been no empirical work testing the assumptions and propositions effectively owing to scarcity of data, unreliable data, and inadequate methodology. In the following chapters additional theoretical explanations are advanced for the causes and shifts in the structure of mortality decline, and a new methodological approach to testing these explanations is applied.

Table 1. Changes Over Time Suggested in the Literature
in Factors Affecting Mortality

	LDCs	MDCs
BEFORE 1880	ECONOMIC DEVELOPMENT	ECONOMIC DEVELOPMENT; IMPROVED LIVING STANDARDS, ESPECIALLY FOOD SUPPLIES
1880-1930	ECONOMIC DEVELOPMENT	PUBLIC HEALTH AND CHEAP HEALTH TECHNOLOGY
1930-1960	CHEAP HEALTH TECHNOLOGY	MODERN MEDICINE
1960-PRESENT	ECONOMIC DEVELOPMENT; RESOURCE DISTRIBUTION	RESOURCE DISTRIBUTION; INDIVIDUALS' LIFE STYLE CHOICES

Notes

1. Omran (1983) describes four basic models of epidemiological transition:

   1.   the classical or Western model, (experienced by most European countries, the United States, and Canada),

   2.   the accelerated variant of the classical model (exemplified by Japan),

   3.   the delayed model (experienced by most LDCs), and

   4.   the transitional variant of the delayed model (Taiwan, Korea, Singapore, Hong Kong, Sri Lanka, Mauritius, Jamaica, and China, all nations which experienced rapid mortality decline, mostly in the 1940s, to levels not reached by most LDCs).

2. Preston (1980) estimates that less than 3% of the total 1972 health expenditure in LDCs was from bilateral or multilateral sources of health aid. However, relatively low-cost international health programs have brought about dramatic mortality reduction in LDCs.

3. Murray (1987) criticized Grosse and Perry's conclusions because they used life expectancy data based on U.N. estimates rather than on solid data. Murray concluded that of all the cross-national mortality data available, the *U.N. Population Trends and Policies Monitoring Reports* and the U.S. Bureau of the Census *World Population* series are superior.

4. The annual rate of mortality improvement in Africa was .43 years for the 1950s to the 1960s, .53 years for the 1960s to the 1970s, and .61 years for the 1970s to the 1980s.

Chapter 4

THEORY AND HYPOTHESES

A. INTRODUCTION

Almost all mortality research by demographers, sociologists, and economists is descriptive and practical in orientation. There is considerable concern for policy application of research results for humanitarian reasons and as a means of expediting fertility reduction. It is felt that the more we know about factors affecting mortality, the better the chances are of speeding the demographic transition, achieving stable populations through mortality reduction and fertility reduction.

Most of the mortality research described in Chapter 2 was intended only to describe and explain mortality patterns. Those analyses are empiricist in character: they focus on amassing observations and generalizing from those observations. Though demographic variables are considered in the context of demographic transition theory, that "theory" is really only a collection of empirical generalizations, or a model, or at best a simple knowledge structure (Cohen 1980). A scientific theory consists of assumptions, scope conditions, derived propositions, primitive terms, and defined terms. Ideally, theory assists in organizing ideas, guides investigation, and generates explanations and predictions. What seems an incredibly complex set of relationships and processes may be thoroughly clarified by analysis based on theory.

Empirical observations should be used, among other things, to test hypotheses derived from theory. Theory and empirical research are closely interrelated.

Demography tends to be concerned with events that occur in a particular space-time context rather than with developing abstract, theoretical, scientific knowledge. In general, demography tends to follow the historical orientation rather than the generalizing orientation. The goal of the historical orientation is to understand a phenomenon; the goal of the generalizing orientation is to evaluate theories. The latter process may be useful in producing scientific knowledge but not always immediately useful in solving practical problems (Cohen 1980), whereas it is clear that understanding of phenomena can facilitate policy development.

It is not surprising that demography has focused on accurate measurement of population trends, forecasting, and description of data. The pressure on scholars to provide practical answers to social problems is great. Nevertheless, in the long run it would be more productive to be concerned with both theorizing and developing information to assist policy formulation.

Demographers' concern with policy relevance and practical application of research usually causes them to adopt the historical orientation. However, that orientation leads to descriptions of specific situations which are less likely to apply to a new situation than are the results of the generalizing orientation (Cohen 1980). Perhaps it would be most useful to accept both the historical and generalizing viewpoints to broaden understanding of complex events. The generalizing orientation and resulting scientific theory should be added to demographic investigation to make the formulation of problems meaningful, and demographic research should play a more important role in providing data for testing theories.

The observed relationships between mortality and its antecedents can be used to test predictions derived from sociological theory. The study of mortality patterns can certainly be enhanced by viewing those patterns as consequences of socioeconomic phenomena predicted by theoretical formulations. More important, the observed patterns can be used in the systematic process of theory construction, the formulation and evaluation of theory. This will facilitate understanding of new situations as they arise.

B. ALTERNATIVE THEORIES OF SOCIOECONOMIC DEVELOPMENT

1. Modernization Theory

One long-standing view in social sciences is that economic development leads to overall modernization and "progress." Development is seen as an evolutionary process: nations grow healthier and mature as they modernize. Internal changes in a society associated with modernization help citizens when benefits from their society's economic development "trickle down." According to this view, a main cause of mortality reduction is economic development with its accompanying improvements in living standards. Economic and technological developments allow challenges to traditional fatalistic acceptance of high infant and child mortality. Societies begin to fight disease and death aggressively. Much of the literature discussed in Chapters 2 and 3 assumes that a major cause of mortality reduction, past and present, is modernization or economic development. This line of reasoning leads to the first hypothesis:

Hypothesis 1: Economic development reduces mortality.

This approach to explaining mortality reduction emphasizes factors endogenous to a society. For a more complete understanding of the process, one must also recognize mortality-reducing influences which are exogenous to a society, especially public health technologies. Other theoretical perspectives describe such exogenous factors and their introduction into societies and suggest different explanations for mortality reduction in the modern world. World system theory and dependency theory have implications which lead to additional hypotheses.

2. World System and Dependency Theories

Some world system theorists assert that in modern times a world culture consisting of international norms, roles, organizations, and institutions has developed and spread (Meyer et al. 1975; Meyer and Hannan 1979; Meyer 1980). Societies have grown increasingly similar as a consequence of diffusion of this world culture. Dependency theory, closely related to world system theory, describes the relationships among groups and among nations in terms of stratification, unequal economic exchange, and exploitation. Both dependency theory and world system theory make specific statements regarding different patterns of economic development, resource distribution, modernization, the rise of strong nation-states, the relationships between MDCs and LDCs, and the reasons for these differences.

World system theory and dependency theory are discussed in detail in the following sections. These theories provide the basis for hypotheses about causes of mortality decline in both LDCs and MDCs. They focus on the impact of national governments and international agencies and help answer Caldwell's (1986b) complaint, ". . . far too little has been done to incorporate into both mortality and demographic transition theory the intervention of national governments and international agencies and the accompanying sentiments and ideologies that have made such action possible. They tend to be treated as exogenous, as something artificial and determined, in contrast to the more natural transitions of the West. Nevertheless, comprehensive theory should aim at embracing the whole picture."

a. *World System Theory*

World system theorists focus on the effects of an almost universal set of values and beliefs about economic, social, and political processes that exists within nations. They suggest that international consensus develops about desirable structures and goals for human groups. This consensus diffuses widely throughout the world, facilitated by increasing cultural similarities. The consensus, or "world culture," places high values on economic development and its components: strong nation-states, universal education, mobilized citizens, individual modernity, and national economic prosperity. The degree to which a nation-state has adopted these values and goals affects its status in the international stratification system. National elites in colonies and LDCs are socialized into the viewpoint of the world system and pursue it aggressively. The modernity of a society is sometimes measured in terms of acceptance of world system norms by its citizens (Inkeles and Smith 1974), and those areas with lowest status (the most "backward") are those which have adopted relatively few of them.

Among the values of the world are those assigning importance to individuals as agents of the state and believing that the state should assume concern for its citizens' welfare. It is argued that because the state relies on individual productivity to achieve economic and social modernization, universal education and public health programs should be created. This explanation leads to

Hypothesis 2: Availability of health care reduces mortality.

In providing programs to enhance its citizens' welfare, the state gains world respectability or status. Leaders, however, to maintain a respectable image in the international community, may suppress or manipulate socioeconomic data on citizens' welfare and the extent of their nation's welfare programs.

Colonial powers introduced education and health programs into their colonies (though sometimes their initial purpose may have been to safeguard the health of colonial administrators). On gaining independence, new nations in Latin America, Asia, and Africa were left to pursue the goals of the world system into which their leaders had been socialized. If education and health systems were not already widespread within an independent nation-state, they might have been imported from states more incorporated into the world system and/or from the international organizations founded to integrate peripheral nations into the world system. It is hypothesized that

Hypothesis 3: International health aid reduces mortality.

The world system perspective predicts extensive diffusion of education, health services, and medical technology into countries low in the world stratification system from countries higher in that system (Meyer, et al. 1975). Availability of health care within nation-states should be directly related to degree of world system involvement. Those who have debated whether mortality reduction results from economic development or from public health interventions often overlook the possibility that both may be influenced by degree of incorporation into the world system.

Improved communications among nations contribute to the transfer of ideals, including the humanitarian belief that social resources should be allocated to improve the welfare of individuals. They also facilitate transfer of medical and scientific technology. According to Preston (1980), the MDCs' contributions to mortality reduction in LDCs have not been primarily financial. Instead, they have included development of low cost health measures exploitable on a large scale, demonstration of their effectiveness in relatively small areas, training and provision of personnel and occasionally the initiation of a large-scale program, the major cost of which is often absorbed by the recipient country. Essentially, this amounts to diffusion of ideas and skills, and diffusion occurs more effectively when communications improve.

It is clear from the above discussion that mortality reduction is to some extent a result of world system involvement: it is a consequence of diffusion of the world culture and an empirical indicator of convergence of cultures. World system involvement results in economic development, health care availability, and international health aid, which in turn induce mortality reduction.[1]

Hypothesis 4:   World system involvement leads to mortality reduction.

As LDCs enter the world system and that system expands,

Hypothesis 5:   Mortality levels in MDCs and LDCs converge over time.

Diffusion makes world culture increasingly homogeneous and uniform. Unless something intervenes to prevent complete equalization of mortality levels, diffusion should result in reduction of cross-national mortality differentials until all countries are incorporated into the world system. Dependency theorists propose that often something does intervene to prevent equalization of mortality.

b. *Dependency Theory*

Lenski (1966) argued that as societies changed from hunting-and-gathering to horticultural to agrarian in the process of socioeconomic modernization, the concentration of resources and rewards became more inequitable. This was because the surpluses produced were increasingly retained by those in power. When societies began to industrialize, the increasing division of labor caused both a diffusion of power and privilege and an increase in specialization. Because they possessed valuable skills, people who were otherwise underprivileged could acquire political power with which to effect some redistribution of rewards.

Lenski's theory can be extended to predict overall mortality reduction and decreases in class differences in mortality as societies industrialize and develop economically. Preston (1978b) interprets evidence from a series of studies of child mortality in nine Latin American countries as showing that as development proceeds, social class differences in mortality are reduced. His conclusions tend to support this extension of Lenski's theory. Lenski also asserts that redistribution of power and privilege stops short of complete equality, a view supported by Antonovsky's report of retention of a class mortality differential (1967). Adelman and Morris' (1973) analysis of income distribution and economic development appears to confirm Lenski's idea of an inverse relationship between income distribution and economic development in the earlier stages of development, sometimes called "classical" dependency (Bradshaw 1988).

One result of the development of a world system was increasing similarity of form (institutions and other social structures) among societies without increasing equality of outcomes (Meyer and Hannan 1979). Expanded states, education, urbanization, and industrialization became widespread, but the inherent stratification of the world system (an economic division of labor) promoted international inequality and increased inequality within societies. This has been called "dependent development" by Bradshaw (1988). Specialization of MDCs in more profitable economic enterprises and of LDCs in less profitable ones led to a relationship of economic dependence (Rubinson 1976). Adelman and Morris' (1973) finding that diffusion of technology may increase economic inequalities within LDCs can be interpreted as support for the prediction from dependency theory that foreign economic penetration and control over economic activities increase economic inequality within nations (Rubinson 1976).

Opportunities for diffusion of ideals and technologies resulted from the economic dependence of LDCs on MDCs which ensued from the creation of a world system. Economic dependence and indebtedness also drained resources which could have been used by LDCs to improve living standards and to develop economically (Chase-Dunn 1975; Gobalet and Diamond 1979; Sell and Kunitz 1986-7). This suggests that creation of a world system and the resulting pattern of economic dependence resulted in international inequality of mortality levels after the initial convergence discussed in connection with Hypothesis 4. Therefore, even after development of a world system and some convergence of life expectancies,

Hypothesis 6:   Inequalities in mortality levels between MDCs and LDCs persist.

Though forces to standardize world culture produce agreement on the desirability of improving living standards, including reducing morbidity and mortality, the MDC-LDC division of labor makes it difficult for all citizens in LDCs to achieve these ideals. Ironically, though diffusion of values mitigates in favor of equality, dependency tends to perpetuate inequality. Furthermore, economic inequality between nations increases disparities of mortality within dependent LDCs so that mortality reduction is slowed (Hout 1980; Sell and Kunitz 1986-7), as well as fertility reduction (London 1988). According to this argument, economic dependence leads to inequitable distribution of resources so that

Hypothesis 7:   Economic dependence hinders mortality decline.

Dependency theory suggests that one reason the recent mortality reduction processes in MDCs and LDCs have differed is that dependence made it difficult for LDCs to develop enough to achieve the type of extensive redistribution of resources necessary to effect additional mortality declines. Where efforts to provide mass education, health care and food have occurred (in Sri Lanka, Cuba, and Kerala), greater mortality reduction has been achieved than in other nations at similar levels of per capita income (Preston 1978b; Caldwell 1986a). Other countries have experienced great economic growth with comparatively modest mortality improvements in recent decades because they have only recently begun to convert income gains into social and economic progress. This leads to

Hypothesis 8:   Equality of resource distribution within a nation-state reduces mortality.

The distribution of resources within nations may be an increasingly important factor in future mortality reduction, as suggested in Chapters 2 and 3.

The expansion of the world system, therefore, leads to diffusion of technologies and motivations to extend life expectancy but also causes socioeconomic differentiation of nation-states. This results in continued mortality differentials within LDCs and between LDCs and MDCs.

C. TIME PATTERNS

The thresholds or stages of mortality change described in Chapter 3 generally coincide with phases described in world system theory. Rokkan (1975) described a four-stage process of nation-state building in which the first stage is state-building (political, economic, and cultural unification of elites within a society). The second stage is nation-building (incorporating the masses into the system through education and development of identity with the total political system). The third stage is participation-building (bringing the masses into active participation in political processes). The fourth stage is redistribution of resources (including development of welfare systems and economic redistribution through taxation). His chronology for Western Europe describes Phase 1 occurring from about 1500 until 1700, Phase 2 from about 1700 until 1850, Phase 3 from about 1850 until 1910, and Phase 4 since about 1910. The majority of political systems in Latin America, Eastern Europe, Asia, and Africa experienced the process rapidly because much of it was imposed by or imported from Western Europe during colonization. According to Rokkan, the colonists typically left their colonies' administrative machinery with Phases 2, 3, and possibly 4 coinciding. The postcolonial LDCs were left in various stages of economic and cultural dependence on the core nation-states of Western Europe. They had neither the time nor the internal organization to develop institutions and technologies of their own, so they imported them even after independence. Hence, education, health care, family structure, political organization, and sometimes even religion follow European models in most former colonies today.

The date 1880 suggested in the literature as the approximate time western nations' mortality levels began to be influenced more by public health measures than by economic development is the midpoint of Rokkan's dates for Phase 3. Actually, some Western European nation-states began to develop welfare systems by the late 1800s, and 1880 should probably be viewed as the time public health measures began to dominate in mortality reduction in western nations. Similarly, 1930 may be viewed as the beginning of most important mortality reductions from public health inputs in LDCs.

Tilly (1975) described similar stages in the general move toward a worldwide, culturally homogeneous state system. This move consisted, first, of the formation of a few early nation-states amid a great variety of other political structures in Western Europe. Much of Western Europe was formed into distinct nation-states by 1700, and by then the second main process of developing the modern system had begun. Political and economic domination were then extended from their European base to much of the rest of the world through creation of client states and colonies. Through a process of rebellion and international agreement, these gradually became formally autonomous states so that the state system now includes almost all of the world. At the same time, cultural homogeneity increased because Europe exported its ideologies as well as its political system.

As a nation is incorporated into the world system, the state expands: its power is increased and its functions are augmented. The modern state's monopoly of coercive power and its control of resources are channeled by its acceptance of the nearly universal world value system into efforts to improve its citizens' quality of life. Therefore,

Hypothesis 9:   State strength results in mortality reduction.

Increasingly, nation-states become socialistic and welfare-oriented (Meyer 1980). Among the functions often assumed by the state is provision of medical care. Part of the modern world's culture is the belief that individual welfare and progress should be furthered by the state. Even though this valuation of the individual may be mythical (Meyer 1980) or cynical, the process of increasing state strength leads to efforts to reduce mortality.

D. SUMMARY

Mortality trends may be explained in terms of conventional development or modernization theory and/or in terms of implications of world system and dependency theories. Perhaps more important, results of empirical investigation of mortality can be used to test parts of those theories and to aid in their development.

Development or modernization theory assumes that economic development leads to various changes and improvements in living standards for individuals, including reduced morbidity and mortality. World system and dependency theory derivations which are particularly relevant to explanation of mortality trends are those that suggest world system expansion results in

1. convergence of ideologies,
2. economic development,
3. diffusion of health technology,
4. international health aid programs,
5. inequalities between classes of nations and within LDCs, and
6. increased state strength.

Mortality patterns should show evidence of these processes. Specifically as world culture spreads, health technologies are diffused and the mortality levels of nations become increasingly similar. As nation-states evolve and states become stronger, mortality reduction accelerates. As classes of nations (MDCs and LDCs) develop, inequalities in mortality levels and patterns of mortality change emerge. Therefore, the relationship between mortality levels in MDCs and LDCs depends upon the stage of development of the world system and the position of each nation within that system.

Development of a cumulative research program to investigate systematically these possible causes of mortality reduction should provide more knowledge than the previous historical, atheoretical analyses. As the theory-based research program proceeds, mortality research (and perhaps demographic research in general) can be used to advance theory. Chapter 5 describes the measures and methods used to test the hypotheses based on these theories.

Notes

1. As a country enters the world system, it is likely to develop the ability and the motivation to begin to collect data (including vital statistics) and make them available to other countries and to international organizations like the League of Nations, United Nations, World Health Organization, and World Bank. Hence, data availability is one sign of world system involvement.

Chapter 5

METHODS AND MEASURES

The methods used in previous research to assess causes of mortality reduction have been inadequate. Most studies have been cross-sectional. They studied life expectancy or infant mortality and its correlates at only one point in time (U.N. 1980; Yang and Pendleton 1980: Pendleton and Yang 1985). This approach obviously cannot indicate causes of change over time. Neither can it explicitly reflect the effects of social and economic factors on later mortality levels.

Preston (1976) compared results from cross-sectional regression analyses for two points in time, 1930 and 1960. He performed regression analyses using change in life expectancy at birth (1940-1970) as his dependent variable and a variety of change scores and ordinary measures for 1940, including 1940 life expectancy, as independent variables (Preston 1980). Sagan and Afifi (1978) also used this method, with change in infant mortality rate 1950-1970 as their dependent variable. This approach to explaining mortality trends is inappropriate, since use of a change score as the dependent variable may yield biased estimates of the effects of the independent variables on the dependent variable (Hannan 1979; Gravelle and Backhouse 1987).

A. PANEL ANALYSIS

When the researcher's goal is to assess causes of change over time, panel analysis is a better method than comparing cross-sections or use of a change score as the dependent variable. In panel analysis, the dependent variable is regressed on the independent variable at an earlier point in time and on the earlier value of the dependent variable. [1] is the basic panel analysis equation:

$$Y'_{t_2} = a + b_1 Y_{t_1} + b_2 X_1 + \ldots + b_n X_n + u \qquad [1]$$

This provides a longitudinal, cross-sectional analysis of the effects of earlier independent variables on the dependent variable. Though panel analysis has some shortcomings, it is superior for assessing causation over time to most techniques used in the past by researchers studying mortality.

In panel analysis it is important to select an appropriate time period, or lag, over which the independent variables will have sufficient time to act on the dependent variable. When life expectancy is the dependent variable, an appropriate lag period might be one or two decades. This allows time for economic development, health care, and other measures to reduce mortality rates for older groups from causes which are cumulative, wasting, or take time to kill. When infant mortality is the dependent variable, the lag could be shorter since infant mortality would respond rapidly to improved environmental conditions.

Because historical data for several independent variables were available at 20 year intervals, that lag period was selected for historical panel analyses for 1890-1910, 1910-1930, 1930-1950, and 1950-1970. Ten year lag periods were used for 1950-1960, 1960-1970, and 1970-1978 (1978 was the most recent estimate of life expectancy available when these analyses were performed).

The basic analytical method used here is multiple regression analysis of panels with ordinary least squares estimation. This provides a methodological improvement over earlier studies. One potential problem of this method is autocorrelation, which may yield biased and inconsistent estimators. This results from non-independence of disturbance terms (Hannan 1979). The Durbin-Watson test for autocorrelation was used with indecisive results: it is not possible to decide whether autocorrelation is a problem. Therefore, ordinary least squares was judged to be an adequate estimator at this stage of investigation. Future investigations should attempt to utilize other types of estimators.

Multicollinearity, high intercorrelation of the independent variables, is also often a problem with panel analysis of processes associated with socioeconomic development. Multicollinearity tends to inflate the standard errors of regression coefficients, making it more difficult to achieve statistically significant results. The variables included in each regression equation were selected to minimize this problem: highly correlated measures of independent variables were not included in the same equation. With one exception, each analysis includes at most the lagged dependent variable, a measure of economic development, and a measure of one of the other independent variables.

The basic panel analysis equation [1] is based on an assumption of linearity: it assumes that independent variables exert the same influences at every level of mortality. However, as others have pointed out (Schultz 1976; Preston 1980; Gravelle and Backhouse 1987), this is not a valid assumption. The results of ordinary panel analysis discussed later (in Chapter 7) must therefore be viewed skeptically, as should earlier researchers' results based on assumptions of linearity. Chapter 8 describes a nonlinear model of the process of life expectancy rising over time and presents some results from its application.

B. MEASURES

Measures of dependent and independent variables and their sources are summarized in Table 2. Most measures were chosen because they were available for the largest number of nations at the greatest number of times, and they conceptualized the variables reasonably well.

1. Mortality

There are several possible measures of the dependent variable, mortality, including infant mortality rate, child mortality rate, and life expectancy.[1] Infant mortality is highly variable: it was estimated to be

more than five times higher in the LDCs than in the MDCs in the early
1980s (U.N. 1984). This variation would make it a useful dependent
variable. Infant mortality (particularly postneonatal infant mortality)
would probably be the measure most sensitive to the distribution of the
benefits of development and the level of inequality within a society.
Unfortunately infant mortality data often are unreliable (though
according to the I.R.G. (1979), infant and child mortality estimates
derived from estimates in LDCs may often be better than mortality
data for older groups). Increasingly, the relationships between infant
mortality, other age specific mortality rates, and life expectancy at birth
is being studied (Arriaga 1984; Pollard 1988). There is also an attempt
to determine the effects of age specific death rates and patterns of
causes of death on mortality in general.

Female life expectancy might be a better measure of the dependent
variable than total (combined male and female) life expectancy or male
life expectancy because there is some evidence that the effects of social
inequality are greater upon women (Antonovsky 1967). At earlier
stages of development, females are less likely to receive the benefits of
education and nontraditional labor force participation than men. In
LDCs, female life expectancy may be shorter than male life expectancy.
Eventually women achieve greater gains in life expectancy from development than do men, particularly as fertility falls. Women may have
life expectancies nearly a decade longer than men in MDCs. Hence
female life expectancy has greater variation and would be a more
sensitive mortality measure than male life expectancy. Furthermore,
the correlations between female life expectancy and measures of development and inequality are slightly higher than those for male life
expectancy. However, life expectancy data by sex are sometimes
unavailable, especially for LDCs and for historic periods.

Expectation of life at birth for the combined male and female
populations is the mortality measure most generally available and is
used here.[2] Life expectancy data were gathered for as many nations as
possible for 1870, 1880, 1890, 1900, 1910, 1920, 1930, 1940, 1950, 1960,
1970, 1978, 1980, 1985, and 1987. United Nations (1979) estimates of
life expectancy for 145 nations for the periods 1950-55 through 1980-85
were also used in some analyses to maximize sample sizes. Infant
mortality data were gathered for 1960, 1970, 1975, and 1977, 1978,
1979, or 1980.

2. Economic Development

Per capita gross national product (GNP) is one of the most frequently-used measures of economic development level, despite many shortcomings including data not being comparable for different countries. It is among the most readily available economic indicators for modern times. Per capita GNP data for 1950, 1960, and 1970 were used for the analyses over ten year lag periods (1950-60, 1960-70, and 1970-78). Because the variable is rather skewed, it was transformed logarithmically.

For the historical analyses using twenty year lag periods, an economic development index created by Boli-Bennett (1976) was used. His index was constructed using factor analysis to combine indicators of economic development at twenty year intervals. For 1870, 1890, and 1910, his index was based on miles of railroad, miles of telegraph line, volume of letter mail, steel production, proportion of school-aged children in primary schools, and proportion of the population in cities with over 20,000 inhabitants. For 1930, 1950, and 1970, his index combined national income, percent of labor force in agriculture, proportions of population living in urban areas, and per capita energy consumption. The two indexes are highly correlated and each is superior to its individual components as a measure of economic development.

In order to clarify mortality trends in countries according to level of economic development and stage in the demographic transition, countries were categorized as MDCs and LDCs. MDCs (also called "West" in Chapter 6) are European nations, Canada, the United States, Iceland, the U.S.S.R., Australia, New Zealand, and Japan. LDCs are all Latin American and African nations and the remaining nations in Asia and Oceania. Preliminary analysis of samples divided according to level of life expectancy gave results virtually identical to those obtained from the more conventional MDC/LDC division used here.

3. Health Care Availability and Health Aid

Ideally, health care availability measures would include indicators of the distribution of hospitals, clinics, doctors, dentists, nurses, midwives, vaccination programs, and public health measures (immunization, clean water supplies and sanitation) throughout each country. To indicate the diffusion of modern medical technology from MDCs to LDCs, one would also wish for data on medical aid from MDCs and international agencies, on the extent of foreign-sponsored or foreign-staffed health programs, and on the proportions of doctors and other medical personnel in LDCs who were trained in more developed nations.

Other possible measures of health care availability include percent of GNP spent by the government on health care. However, there are difficulties resulting from incomparability of national accounting systems: countries use various methods to itemize public health expenditures. For example, health expenditure is not always itemized separately. Government health care spending as a percent of GNP was used in preliminary analyses as a measure of government commitment to health improvement and maintenance programs.

Two major measures of health care availability and international health aid were chosen after extensive examination of available data and coding and preliminary investigations of a variety of measures. These included population per physician, physicians per 10,000 population, nurses per 10,000 population, hospital beds per 10,000 population, percent of population with access to safe water, percent of population served by sewage disposal facilities, and percent of government expenditure which was for health. Data on international health aid by philanthropic organizations, governments, and international organizations were also reviewed.

It was decided to measure health care availability using physicians per 10,000 population. Data were found for 1930, 1950, 1960, and 1970. Unfortunately, adequate data for earlier dates were not located.

Health aid was measured using dollars per 1000 population given for public health by the Rockefeller Foundation from 1913 to 1919 and from 1930 to 1939 and by the World Health Organization in 1950, 1960, and 1970. The Rockefeller Foundation, the leader among philanthropic foundations in public health assistance since its operations in this field began in 1913, contributed a substantial percent of the League of Nations Health Organization's budget. In its early years, the L.N.H.O. received nearly half its very small income from the Rockefeller Foundation (Chisholm 1967). In 1926, the Rockefeller Foundation provided $153,840, which was 65.2% of the League's health budget (Vincent 1927). From 1913 to 1929, nearly $1 million was given to the

L.N.H.O. by the Rockefeller Foundation out of the Foundation's total public health expenditures of over $41 million (Rockefeller Foundation 1934). Unfortunately, the L.N.H.O. apparently did not report its small public health expenditures by country. However, the Rockefeller Foundation's expenditures dwarfed those of the League and every other organization. Since the Foundation reported its expenditures comparatively carefully by year, country, and program, it was decided to use these data. After World War II, the World Health Organization replaced the Rockefeller Foundation as the leading provider of international health aid. Its contributions are reported by country in its annual *Official Records* (W.H.O. 1950-1976), and these data were used for 1950, 1960, and 1970. Neither of the measures selected is ideal, because both the supply of physicians and the amount of health aid can be a reflection of earlier high mortality levels. Efforts to reduce mortality can produce higher levels of both variables, so that it is possible these could appear to have a negative effect on mortality.

4. World System Involvement

World system involvement is measured as Rubinson (1976) suggests, in terms of the value of imports and exports as a percent of the gross domestic product. This measure should give information about the importance of external factors in mortality reduction within nations in the absence of data on actual diffusion of health care technology. World system involvement is hypothesized to lead to lower mortality, both directly and indirectly, through its effects on health care availability, economic development, and receipt of health aid (Hypothesis 4). Data were used for 1890, 1910, 1930, 1950, 1960, and 1970.

5. Economic Dependence

Dependence was measured as investment dependence, the average value over a five year period of debits on investment income, the amount of all income earned by foreign direct and portfolio investment in host countries. This measure (in U.S. dollars) was averaged over time to avoid possible problems of short-term fluctuations, and was

divided by the average population for that five year period to control
for the size of the nation. The measure was transformed logarithmically to reduce the skew of its distribution. Data were used for 1950-1955
and 1960-1965 (I.M.F. 1950-65 and 1972).

6. Equality

The equity of distribution of material and nonmaterial goods within
nations is difficult to measure. Economists often use only distribution
of income as an indicator of equality though even this is not available
for all nations, particularly not for Communist nations and many
LDCs. Intranational income inequality data are notoriously poor
(Hoover 1989).

Income inequality, the extent to which income is distributed in-
equitably in a society, may be measured in several ways. Jain (1975)
describes these methods. One of the most common is the Gini ratio,
the ratio of the area bounded by a Lorenz curve (a plot of the
cumulative percentages of national income received by recipient units,
such as individual wage earners or households) and the area bounded
by a diagonal representing equal income distribution across percentiles
of the population.

The measure of income distribution used here is the proportion of
national income received by the bottom 40% of recipients. This is a
measure of income equality rather than inequality. It is more sensitive
to income distribution in lower socioeconomic groups, which tend to be
both relatively and absolutely disadvantaged in LDCs, than Gini
ratios.[3] Ahluwalia (1974 and 1976) believes this measure to be as
useful as Gini ratios. He summarized these data for a variety of
nations about 1970 (1974). Adelman and Morris (1973) provide similar
data for about 1960. These data are used with the understanding that
they may not be exactly comparable and that it is therefore risky to use
them as time series data.

7. State Strength

Data on state strength available before 1950 include government
revenue per capita. This measure indicates the resources controlled by

the state which can be used to manage its citizens' lives. This measure in constant dollars for 1890, 1910, 1930, 1950, and 1970 was compiled by Boli-Bennett (1976).

A measure which may better reflect state dominance is government revenue as a percent of gross domestic product. It describes the extent to which the state controls economic resources: it indicates the proportion of the economy that is under government domination. This measure is available for many nations after 1950. Data for 1955 and 1970 collected by Rubinson (1976) were used here.

C. SUMMARY

The information in Table 2 summarizes the sources of data for all dependent and independent variables. The analyses for which results are reported in Chapters 6, 7, and 8 were performed using various of these measures, which varied according to the period studied. All sources are cited fully in the References.

Table 2. Sources of Data

Conceptual Variables:	Measures Used:	Sources of Data:
Mortality	expectation of life at birth (combined male and female) in 1870, 1880, 1890, 1900, 1910, 1920, 1930, 1940, 1950, 1950, 1970, 1978, 1980, 1987, 1950-55, 1955-60, 1960-65, 1965-70, 1970-75, 1975-80, 1980-85, 1985-90, 1990-95, 1995-2000, 2000-05, 2005-10, 2010-15, 2015-20, 2020-25	Arriaga 1968 I.B.R.D. 1978, 1979, 1980, 1982, 1989 Keyfitz and Flieger 1971 Preston 1976, 1980 Schultz 1976 Sundbarg 1968 U.N. 1979, 1980, 1986b U.N.D.Y. 1951, 1954, 1957, 1961, 1967, 1974 U.N.S.Y. 1949-50, 1951, 1967
	infant mortality rate in 1960, 1970, and 1977-80	I.B.R.D. 1978, 1979, 1980 U.N. 1981
Economic Development	development index for 1890, 1910, 1930, 1950, 1970	Boli-Bennett 1976
	ln GNP per capita in 1950, 1955, 1960, 1970	I.B.R.D. 1971, 1976
Health Care Availability	physicians per 10,000 population in 1930, 1950, 1960, 1970	I.B.R.D. 1979 L.N. 1924-30 W.H.O. 1973-79
International Health Aid	Rockefeller Foundation public health aid in dollars per 1000 population in 1913-19 and 1930-39	R.F. 1923-26, 1934-42, 1947-50

Table 2. Sources of Data (continued)

Conceptual Variables:	Measures Used:	Sources of Data:
World System Involvement	World Health Organization public health aid in dollars per 1000 population in 1950, 1960, 1970	W.H.O. 1950-76
Economic Dependence	trade as a percent of GDP in 1890, 1910, 1930, 1950, 1960, 1970	Boli-Bennett 1976 I.M.F. 1972
	debits on investment income, averages for 1950-55 and 1960-65	I.M.F. 1950-65, 1972
Equality of Resource Distribution	percent of national income received by bottom 40% of recipients in 1960 and 1970	Adelman and Morris 1973 Ahluwalia 1974
State Strength	government revenue per capita in 1890, 1910, 1930, 1950, 1970	Boli-Bennett 1976
	government revenue as a percent of GDP in 1955 and 1970	I.M.F. 1972

Notes

1. Infant mortality rate is the number of deaths to infants under one
   year of age per 1000 live births in a given year. Child mortality rate
   is another age specific mortality rate: deaths per 1000 children in a
   particular age category (usually ages one to four) in a given year.
   Life expectancy at birth is a hypothetical measure. It is an estimate
   of the average number of years a person can expect to live, based on
   the age specific death rates for a given year.

2. It is recognized that life expectancy data vary in quality. There are
   only a few countries which have relatively complete mortality
   records for the past century. Even today, vital registration is
   incomplete in most LDCs. Particularly in Subsaharan Africa, mortality data are incomplete and out of date (Azefor 1981). This lack
   of data has led some to abandon cross-national mortality research
   and to concentrate on the alternative approach, case studies. There
   are many demographic case studies of specific national and sub-
   national populations, but few regional or global studies. The work
   on which the current monograph is based is more ambitious than
   most, and was undertaken with full understanding of data
   shortcomings and of the risks of attempting to reach conclusions on
   the basis of data which vary in accuracy and availability.

3. Gini ratios summarize income distribution across all groups of
   recipients.

Chapter 6

RESULTS: LIFE EXPECTANCY TRENDS

A. TRENDS

It is clear from the literature that the process of increasing life expectancy has differed in MDCs and LDCs: speed, timing, and causes of increase vary. Examination of life expectancy time trends in MDCs and LDCs show these differences clearly. A series of graphs were prepared using life expectancy data from various sources (see Table 2). Appendix A contains lists of countries included in the samples upon which the graphs were based and maps showing the geographical distribution of those countries.

There have been substantial differences in the rate and timing of improvements in life expectancy in MDCs and LDCs (Figure 2). The data for Figure 2 came from the United Nations publication *World Population Prospects: Estimates and Projections As Assessed in 1984* (1986b). The United Nations estimated mortality levels in MDCs and LDCs for five year periods beginning in 1950. The data for 1980 through 2025 are projections. From 1950 through 1975 life expectancies at birth in MDCs and LDCs became increasingly similar. There clearly was convergence of life expectancies, especially between 1955 and 1965. From a difference of 24.7 years in the early 1950s the gap between MDC and LDC life expectancies narrowed to 16.6 years in the late 1970s and 14.7 years in the early 1980s. The proportion of

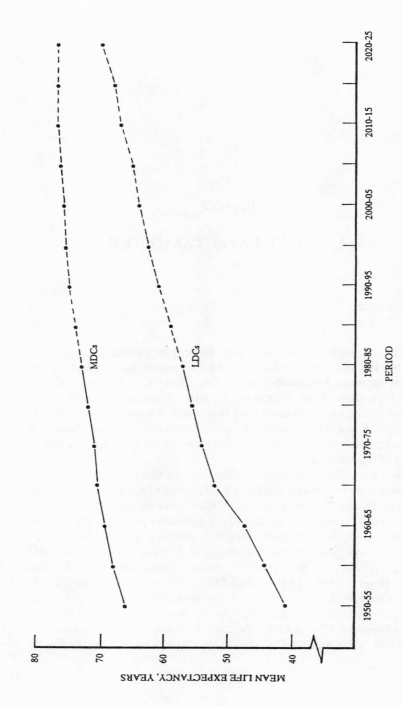

FIGURE 2. LIFE EXPECTANCY IN MDCs AND LDCs
1950-1980 (Estimated) and 1980-2025 (Projected)

MDC life expectancy experienced in LDCs grew from .62 to .77 between the early 1950s and the late 1970s. During the late 1970s, life expectancy differences appeared to be stabilizing with about 17 years' gap between MDCs and LDCs. The United Nations projects continued convergence of life expectancies after 1980, expecting LDCs to experience .90 of MDC levels by 2025, a difference of only 7.7 years. These projections seem overly optimistic when life expectancy trends are examined carefully. It is probably unwarranted to assume that the gap between MDCs and LDCs will gradually be reduced.

Trends in mean life expectancies are shown for constant samples of MDCs and LDCs beginning in 1870, 1890, 1910, 1930, 1950, and 1970 in Figures 3A and 3B. Each sample of countries is larger than those beginning earlier because data are available for more countries recently. Each sample consists of countries for which data are available at all subsequent times, and hence is of constant size.

Examination of mortality trends using progressively larger numbers of constant samples shows that trends are remarkably parallel. Each new sample of MDCs or LDCs exhibits mortality levels and trends close to those samples or MDCs or LDCs for which data became available earlier, though there is more variation from one sample of LDCs to another than among samples of MDCs. Although each country started the mortality transition at a different time, there is little evidence of variation in transition patterns. Regardless of the date mortality data became available, mortality trends seem similar, except that LDCs' rates of improvement tended to be higher than those of MDCs during the same periods between 1940 and 1970.

In both MDCs and LDCs, change in mean life expectancy has been nonlinear (Figures 2, 3A, and 3B). The asymptotic effects of approaching a ceiling in life expectancy different for MDCs and LDCs are somewhat apparent. The MDCs experienced fairly constant rates of improvement in life expectancy from 1870 through 1910, faster improvement until 1950, and somewhat slower improvement during the 1960s and 1970s. The LDCs generally experienced substantial improvement from 1930 (or before, in the older samples) until 1970, and somewhat slower improvement thereafter, though during the 1980s rate of improvement appears to have increased.[1]

Improvement of mean life expectancy over time generally was more rapid for LDCs than for MDCs after 1930. However, life expectancy in the 32 LDCs graphed beginning in 1950 and the 77 graphed beginning

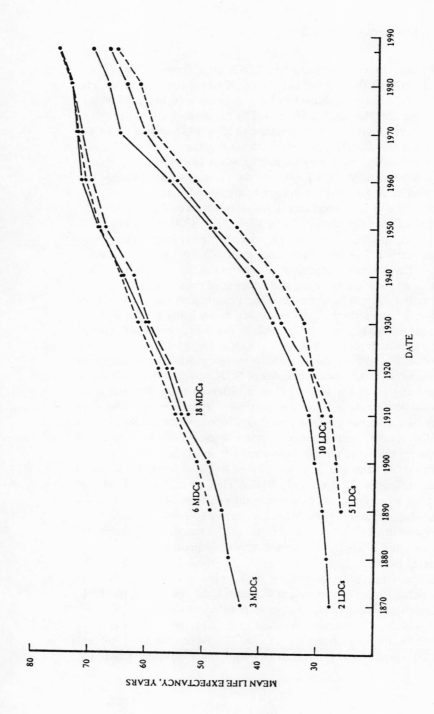

FIGURE 3A.   TRENDS IN LIFE EXPECTANCY IN MDCs AND LDCs
Mean Life Expectancies In Constant Samples
1870-1987, 1890-1987, 1910-1987

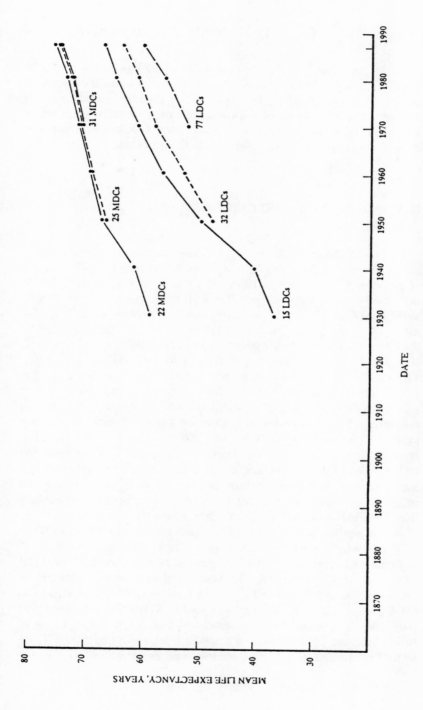

FIGURE 3B. TRENDS IN LIFE EXPECTANCY IN MDCs AND LDCs
Mean Life Expectancies in Constant Samples
1930-1987, 1950-1987, 1970-1987

in 1970 is improving less rapidly than in the smaller groups of LDCs for which data are available earlier. These larger samples include more poor LDCs with shorter life expectancies than the earlier, smaller samples of LDCs. Many of the countries in the samples beginning in 1950 and 1970 are African and other poor LDCs which are just beginning to experience improvements in life expectancy.

B. CONVERGENCE AND CEILINGS

Figures 2, 3A and 3B clearly indicate convergence in mean life expectancies of LDCs and MDCs (until 1970) and partially support Hypothesis 5. After about 1950, MDCs presumably approached the maximum human longevity possible with existing medical technology and life style. Their rates of improvement decreased, while LDCs' mean life expectancies improved rapidly until more recently, when they, too, showed signs of a decreasing improvement rate. Since 1970, there has been little narrowing of the gap between MDCs and LDCs. The LDCs' slowed rate of improvement (compared with that of the 1940s and 50s) probably results from diminished potential for the inexpensive, easy-to-attain mortality reductions from public health measures. The work reviewed in Chapter 3 suggests that convergence in life expectancies in MDCs and LDCs between 1930 and 1960 resulted from the difference between more costly life-prolonging technologies and/or economic development in MDCs and relatively inexpensive public health measures in LDCs. Some of the convergence probably resulted more from MDCs nearing a ceiling of life expectancy than from LDCs experiencing rapid mortality reduction.

A comparison between mean life expectancies in LDCs and MDCs over time which more clearly illustrates this convergence is presented in Figures 4A and 4B. Mean life expectancy in a constant sample of LDCs was divided by mean life expectancy in a constant sample of MDCs at each of a series of points in time to give the proportion of MDCs' mean life expectancy experienced in LDCs at each time. The proportion is graphed for constant samples of countries beginning in 1870, 1890, and 1910 (Figure 4A), and in 1930, 1950, and 1970 (Figure 4B). The samples of countries are the same as those used for Figures

3A and 3B. See Appendix A for lists of countries included in each sample.

Before about 1920, the proportion of MDCs' life expectancy experienced in LDCs was relatively stable at somewhere between .50 and .64. A slight divergence of life expectancies of LDCs and MDCs in the late 1800s and early 1900s may have resulted from mortality reductions in MDCs caused by public health measures, while comparable advances occurred in LDCs only after about 1930. Indeed, the rapid improvement in the LDCs' relative position after 1930 tends to support this explanation from the literature. The greater rate of improvement for all samples between 1930 and 1970 indicates the convergence of life expectancies which is suggested by world system theory and supports Hypothesis 5. Since the 1970s, convergence in the older samples seems to have ceased. This tends to refute Hypothesis 5 but supports Hypothesis 6.

The trends illustrated in Figures 3A, 3B, 4A and 4B reflect a persistent differential in living standards between MDCs and LDCs. This can be interpreted as support for Hypothesis 6. A decreasing rate of convergence since the 1960s is apparent. For example, the group of 15 LDCs graphed from 1930-1987 has experienced a slower rate of convergence with the 22 MDCs in its comparison sample since about 1960. Nine of these 15 LDCs are former colonies in Latin America which, according to Hout (1980), have been victims of dependence. The other six are Asian nations which also have been dependent. Note that the samples graphed beginning in 1950 and 1970 show significantly lower convergence rates than those beginning earlier at comparable life expectancy levels. The LDCs added to the 1950-1987 and 1970-1987 samples are typically poorer and less developed than those for which data were available earlier, though more effective public health interventions may be available to them than was the case for LDCs earlier, and they are experiencing significant convergence.

The low rate of convergence of life expectancies in LDCs and MDCs may be explained in several ways. The socioeconomic inequality of dependency is one possible explanation. There may be a ceiling effect from achievement of maximum gains in life expectancy from inexpensive public health and medical measures. A third possible explanation is recent improvement in MDCs' life expectancies from reductions in diseases of old age or degenerative diseases, particularly

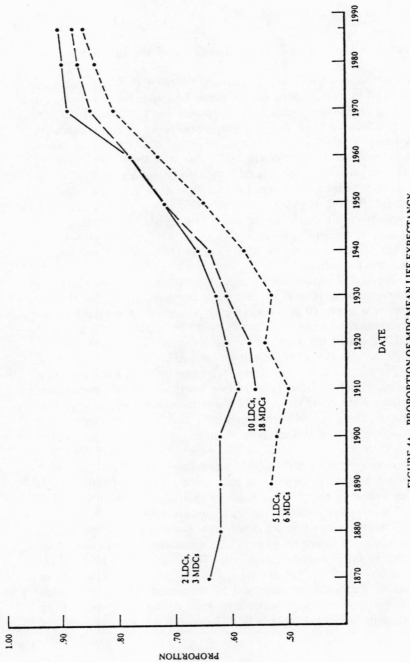

FIGURE 4A. PROPORTION OF MDC MEAN LIFE EXPECTANCY EXPERIENCED IN LDCs

Constant Samples, 1870-1987, 1890-1987, 1910-1987

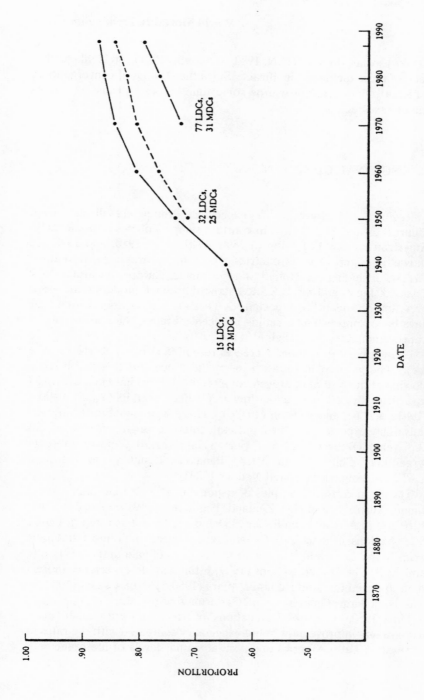

FIGURE 4B. PROPORTION OF MDC MEAN LIFE EXPECTANCY
EXPERIENCED IN LDCs
Constant Samples, 1930-1987, 1950-1987, 1970-1987

cardiovascular disease (U.N. 1980; Crimmins 1981). It is likely that
each of these factors is significant. Since the slowing of convergence is
a recent phenomenon it will be some time before its cause or causes
can be assessed.

C. REGIONAL DIFFERENCES

Regional variations in life expectancy trends are illustrated in
Figures 5A and 5B. Trends in constant samples of Western and Latin
American nations beginning in 1890, 1910, 1930, 1950, and 1970 are
shown in Figure 5A. Countries which today are more developed
("West," including the United States, Canada, Europe, Australia, New
Zealand, Japan and the U.S.S.R.) showed gradual, moderate increases
over time in mean life expectancy. There is some evidence that they
have been approaching a ceiling in recent decades, though the rate of
improvement increased slightly in the 1980s.

Latin American nations' increases resemble a logistic curve (Figure
5A). The greatest increases were in the 1940s and 1950s with some
slowing of the rate of improvement after 1960. This has been discussed
in articles by Accinelli and Mueller (1980), Gwatkin (1980), Palloni
(1981a and b), and Preston (1978b). There were significant differentials in life expectancy at birth in Latin America, ranging in 1980-5 from
50.7 years (Bolivia) and 52.7 years (Haiti) to 70 years or more in
Argentina, Chile, Costa Rica, Panama, Uruguay, and several
Caribbean countries (United Nations 1989).

Trends in constant samples of nations in Asia and Oceania (except
Japan, Australia, and New Zealand) beginning in 1910, 1930, 1950, and
1970 and in Africa beginning in 1950 and 1970 are illustrated in Figure
5B. Nations in Asia and Oceania experienced their most dramatic
gains in the 1920s and 1940s, with slower rates of gain in the 1950s, 60s,
and 70s.[2] The United Nations (1989) estimated life expectancy in East
Asia to have improved from 42.7 years (1950-5) to 68.4 years (1980-5).
This is the largest gain in the LDCs during that period.

Since 1950, the few African nations for which data are available have
had gradual improvement in life expectancy compared with the rates of
increase in Latin America and Asia at similar levels of life expectancy

(40-50 years), though the rate of improvement increased slightly during the 1980s for the 32 nations graphed beginning in 1970. The United Nations (1989) estimated Africa's annual rate of improvement in life expectancy to have been about 0.40 years during the period 1950-5 to 1980-5. This is relatively small compared to other high mortality regions. Eastern, middle, and western Africa were estimated to have life expectancies below 50 years for 1980-5 (substantially lower than life expectancies in northern and southern Africa.

Subsaharan African began to enter the world system only recently and has neither participated in the world culture nor received international health aid to the extent experienced by many Latin American and Asian nations. Africa has the greatest potential for significant further mortality reduction, and inexpensive public health methods may still contribute to future gains. Improved health of infants, children, and young adults will accelerate population growth if Africa follows the Asian and Latin American patterns. In fact, this acceleration has already begun and some of the highest fertility and population growth rates in the world are to be found in Africa. This will aggravate problems of improving living standards and hinder further mortality reduction. However, economic and political problems may prevent Subsaharan Africa from developing economically, absorbing the small amount of international aid tendered, and improving living conditions. As a consequence, their ceiling life expectancy may ultimately be substantially lower than those of the West, Latin America, and Asia. Furthermore the AIDS epidemic may cause life expectancy in Subsaharan African nations to plummet during the 1990s.

The regional patterns illustrated in Figures 5A and 5B provide no evidence of narrowing of the gap in life expectancy in recent decades. Life expectancies in Latin America, Asia and Oceania, and Africa have improved, but so have those in the West. Whereas the 1987 mean life expectancy in countries of the West was 75 years, it was 67 in Latin America, 64 in Asia and Oceania, and 53 in Africa for the countries included in these samples (I.B.R.D. 1989).[3] Overall, the United Nations (1988) found considerable variation in estimated life expectancy at birth for 1985-90: 74 years in MDCs and 59 in LDCs. Africa had the lowest life expectancy (51 years), followed by South Asia (57 years), Oceania excluding Australia and New Zealand (59 years), Latin America (66 years), and East Asia excluding Japan (69 years). Variation within the LDCs was much greater than within the MDCs.

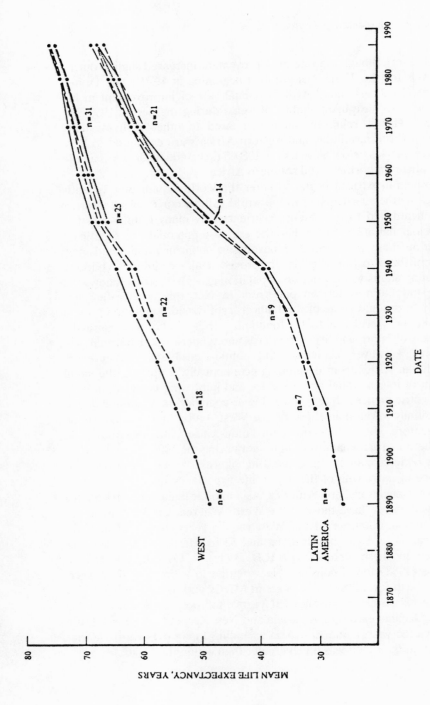

FIGURE 5A. REGIONAL TRENDS IN LIFE EXPECTANCY
Constant Samples of Western and Latin American Nations

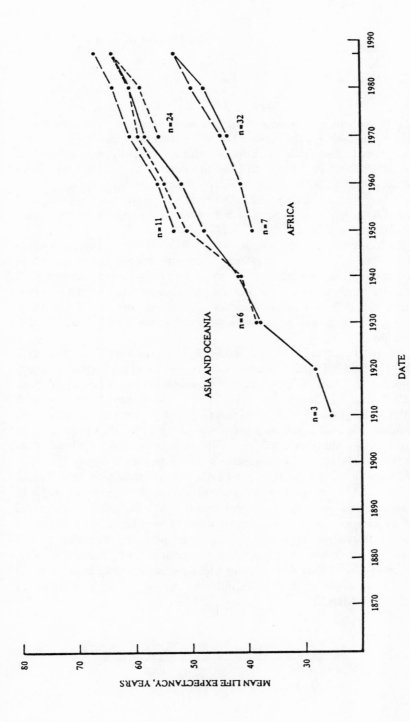

FIGURE 5B. REGIONAL TRENDS IN LIFE EXPECTANCY
Constant Samples of Asian and African Nations

D. SUMMARY

The evidence of distinctive and varied patterns of improvement of life expectancies in the nations for which data are available is striking. Longevity in Latin American and Asian LDCs rapidly approached that of MDCs from 1930-1960. In 1930, life expectancy in LDCs was about 60% of that in MDCs. By 1960 the figure was approximately 75%. Life expectancies in African LDCs began to improve more recently and are still comparatively low, with a long way to go before they approach levels of other LDCs.

Reasons for this improvement in LDCs' life expectancies include expansion of the world system to include ever-larger numbers of societies. The mechanisms of mortality reduction associated with world system expansion are probably international health and development aid, diffusion of public health measures, and establishment of stronger states which organize to implement world humanitarian ideologies.

In recent decades, convergence of life expectancies has slowed. During the 1970s and 1980s a persistent gap developed which was not, apparently, being closed. This is because life expectancies in both MDCs and LDCs are improving at about the same rate. Because MDCs' life expectancies continue to improve there is no reason to assume that LDCs will ever enjoy the levels attained in MDCs. Life expectancy ceilings in LDCs may ultimately be substantially lower than those in MDCs. Convergence of life expectancies may be upon different levels for MDCs and LDCs. There may also be different classes of LDCs: those with higher maximum life expectancies (Latin America and parts of Asia) and those with lower ones (Africa and other parts of Asia). Earlier entry into the world system and onset of the demographic transition is probably positively correlated with eventual attainment of higher living standards and greater longevity. Chapters 7 and 8 explore reasons life expectancies have improved and why there might ultimately be different ceilings of life expectancy in LDCs and MDCs.

Notes

1. The apparent significant increase in rate of improvement of life expectancy in both MDCs and LDCs during the 1980s may result partly from some of the World Bank's (I.B.R.D.'s) estimates for life expectancy being linear interpolations of earlier life expectancy estimates (Murray 1987). Various experts believe that life expectancy is increasing less rapidly than before in many MDCs and LDCs (see Chapters 2 and 3).

2. The three Asian nations' gains in the 1920s resulted largely from improvements in public health in Sri Lanka and the Philippines (Heiser 1936).

3. See *Levels and Trends of Mortality since 1950*, a joint study of the United Nations and World Health Organization, for a detailed discussion of regional mortality patterns (U.N. 1982). The volume includes separate chapters for MDCs, Africa, Asia, and Latin America. Each chapter includes discussions of general levels and trends of mortality, age and sex patterns, and mortality differentials associated with location, ethnicity, and religion.

Chapter 7

RESULTS OF PANEL ANALYSIS

As mentioned in Chapter 5, we assume that mortality changes linearly over time when performing multiple regression analysis for panels using [1] (p. 42). It is quite clear from the results described in Chapter 6 that this assumption is probably invalid. However, because it is desirable to compare a conventional model with a potentially better model, the current chapter reports results of analyses based on assumptions of linearity. Chapter 8 presents a nonlinear model and some results from its application to the same data used in this chapter.

A. RESULTS

Hypothesis 1 states that economic development reduces mortality and therefore improves life expectancy. To test this, life expectancy was regressed on its lagged (earlier) value and on the index of economic development twenty years earlier. In Table 3 results from these regressions are reported which partially support Hypothesis 1 and give further evidence indicating a ceiling effect (nonlinear relationship) of the impact of economic development on life expectancy. In MDCs effects of economic development were never significant, but were positive during the periods 1890-1910 and 1910-1930. After 1930, they

Table 3

Effect of Economic Development on Life Expectancy
Linear Model

Period	Sample	n	Life Expectancy at Beginning of Period			Index of Economic Development			Constant
			b	(S.E.b)	Beta	b	(S.E.b)	Beta	
1890–1910	LDCs	5	.924	(.312)	.913	.214	(1.39)	.047	5.02
"	MDCs	5	1.17	(.399)	1.37	2.11	(1.85)	.537	-3.79
1910–1930	LDCs	8	1.50	(.333)	.884***	-.977	(1.46)	-.131	-9.78
"	MDCs	15	.886	(.112)	.936***	.292	(.661)	.052	13.07
1930–1950	LDCs	14	.601	(.196)	.688***	-.660	(1.23)	-.120	25.18
"	MDCs	27	.543	(.085)	.807***	-.155	(.865)	-.023	35.11
1950–1970	LDCs	25	.822	(.123)	.749***	2.92	(1.12)	.293***	20.67
"	MDCs	23	.477	(.058)	.882***	-.111	(.265)	-.045	30.39

*** p < .01

were negative. This suggests that life expectancy is approaching a ceiling in the most developed countries: recent gains in life expectancy have been made mostly by the less developed MDCs. On the other hand, significant positive effects of economic development on life expectancy were found for LDCs from 1950-1970. LDCs have not exhausted the potential for development to produce improvements in life expectancy.

Hypothesis 2 states that availability of health care increases life expectancy. The findings indicated in Table 3 are reinforced by the information presented in Table 4, which reports the results of regressing life expectancy on economic development, health care availability, and life expectancy ten and twenty years earlier. The effects of economic development on life expectancy were positive. These results of the regressions reported in Table 4 do not support Hypothesis 2, however: physicians per 10,000 population ought to have a positive effect on life expectancy, and none of the significant effects are positive.[1]

Part B of Table 4 indicates shifts in the relative importance of the effects of economic development and health care availability on life expectancy. In the 30 MDCs sampled, the effects of health care were insignificant between 1950-55 and 1960-65 but became significantly negative after 1960-65. This suggests a ceiling effect for the impact of health care on life expectancy. The effects of economic development were significantly negative from 1950-55 to 1960-65 but not thereafter.

In LDCs, health care availability had significant negative effects from 1950-55 to 1960-65 and from 1960-65 to 1970-75 but were not significant (though still negative) in the most recent period. Effects of economic development shifted from negative and insignificant from 1950-55 until 1960-65 to positive and significant during the later periods. This finding supports the assumption discussed in Chapter 3 that in recent decades, economic development has increasingly contributed to life expectancy gains.

Hypothesis 3 states that international health aid results in increased life expectancy. Table 5 presents the results of regressing life expectancy on earlier values of economic development, health aid, and life expectancy. The results reported in Parts A and B of Table 5 do not support Hypothesis 3: when international health aid is statistically significant, its effects on life expectancy are negative. However, this suggests that the linear model is inappropriate here because health aid inputs are supposed to have the greatest impact on life expectancy early

Table 4

Effect of Health Care on Life Expectancy
Linear Model

Part A: Twenty-Year Periods

Period	Sample	n	Life Expectancy at Beginning of Period	Index of Economic Development	Physicians per 10,000 Population	Constant
1930-1950	LDCs	7	1.22 (.438)1.20 *	-6.09 (4.12)-.544	-.258 (.721)-.121	7.51
"	MDCs	16	.419 (.130) .693***	-1.07 (1.49)-.188	.264 (.351) .194	41.81
1950-1970	LDCs	25	.803 (.159) .732***	2.88 (1.15) .290***	.047 (.234) .029	21.41
"	MDCs	16	.586 (.079) .949***	.568 (.408) .184	-.151 (.116)-.187	32.62
			b (S.E.b) Beta	b (S.E.b) Beta	b (S.E.b) Beta	

Part B: Ten-Year Periods

Period	Sample	n	Life Expectancy Beginning of Period	ln GNP per capita	Physicians 10,000 Population	Constant
1950/55-1960/65	LDCs	56	1.07 (.035)1.04 ***	-.694 (.973)-.022	-.167 (.079)-.063***	4.35
	MDCs	30	.645 (.079)1.12 ***	-1.92 (.868)-.298***	.048 (.065) .062	32.23
1960/65-1970/75	LDCs	56	.987 (.027)1.02 ***	1.22 (.768) .045*	-.203 (.062)-.089***	3.14
	MDCs	30	.855 (.086)1.04 ***	-.798 (.718)-.112	-.136 (.049)-.215***	15.59
1970/75-1978	LDCs	56	.915 (.031) .954***	1.45 (.853) .061**	-.035 (.061)-.018	3.69
	MDCs	30	.962 (.090) .024***	-.047 (.730)-.006	-.083 (.038)-.151**	5.20
			b (S.E.b) Beta	b (S.E.b) Beta	b (S.E.b) Beta	

* p < .10
** p < .05
*** p < .01

Table 5

Effect of International Health Aid on Life Expectancy and Infant Mortality, Linear Model

Part A: Twenty-Year Periods

Period	Sample	n	Life Expectancy at Beginning of Period	Index of Economic Development	Rockefeller Foundation Aid per 1000 pop.	Constant
1910-1930	LDCs	8	1.39 (.376) .817**	-.426 (1.67)-.057	.008 (.010) .190	-6.62
"	MDCs	15	.894 (.115) .944***	.481 (.717) .086	-.068 (.089)-.093	12.72
1930-1950	LDCs	14	.581 (.212) .665***	-.762 (1.31)-.139	.015 (.041) .090	25.53
"	MDCs	27	.548 (.087) .815***	-.228 (.879)-.033	.017 (.023) .091	34.56

					WHO Aid per 1000 pop.	
1950-1970	LDCs	25	.958 (.129) .951***	1.78 (.952) .203**	-.179 (.100)-.234**	14.89
"	MDCs	25	.504 (.062) .948***	-.384 (.330)-.150	-.069 (.070)-.138	37.95

Part B: Ten-Year Periods

				ln GNP per capita		
1950-1960	LDCs	23	.788 (.121) .764***	9.83 (3.17) .335***	-.160 (.098)-.172*	-4.65
"	MDCs	22	.706 (.130) .940***	-.922 (1.51)-.101	.002 (.080) .004	24.39
1960-1970	LDCs	43	.860 (.061) .893***	3.16 (2.06) .097*	-.004 (.022)-.009	4.49
"	MDCs	26	.615 (.097) .807***	.969 (1.06) .119	-.002 (.065)-.003	25.81
1970-1978	LDCs	76	.810 (.047) .860***	3.01 (1.22) .123***	-.010 (.005)-.058***	6.52
"	MDCs	30	.756 (.132) .815***	.394 (1.26) .044	.044 (.087) .056	17.53

Part C: Infant Mortality Rate, Ten-Year Periods

Period	Sample	n	b (S.E.b) Beta	b (S.E.b) Beta	b (S.E.b) Beta	Constant
1960-1970	LDCs	34	.607 (.068) .809***	-16.22 (11.49)-.124	-.204 (.129)-.110*	56.65
"	MDCs	26	.717 (.047)1.06 ***	4.62 (3.30) .099	.138 (.154) .039	-15.12
1970-1977/80	LDCs	42	.890 (.145) .778***	-9.56 (16.46)-.072	.023 (.134) .016	19.02
	MDCs	31	.530 (.052) .846***	-4.90 (2.73)-.155**	-.008 (.005)-.087*	18.93

* $p < .10$
** $p < .05$
*** $p < .01$

in the process of mortality reduction. The results reported in Part C of Table 5 do provide some support for Hypothesis 3, because the significant effect for W.H.O. aid on 1970 and 1978 infant mortality rates are negative.

Hypothesis 4 states that world system involvement results in improved life expectancy. Part A of Table 6 presents results from panel analysis of the effects of economic development and trade as a percent of gross domestic product (GDP) on life expectancy for the periods 1950-1960, 1960-1970, and 1970-1978 in LDCs and MDCs. These results do not support Hypothesis 4: in the one instance that trade as a percent of GDP is statistically significant, in MDCs from 1970-1978, its effect is negative. Diffusion of medical technology and health-benefitting developments (as a result of world system involvement) might have become less important before World War II, even before the widespread use of antibiotics. The results reported in Part B of Table 6 do provide some support for Hypothesis 4, since the effect of 1960 world system involvement on 1970 infant mortality rate in LDCs was significantly negative.

Hypothesis 7 states that economic dependence has a negative effect on life expectancy. Table 7 presents results from regressing life expectancy on earlier values of investment dependence per capita, economic development, and life expectancy. The table indicates that investment dependence per capita had insignificant negative effects on life expectancy over the period 1950-1960 in both LDCs and MDCs, and in LDCs during the following decade. In MDCs, dependence had a slightly significant (p < .25) positive effect on life expectancy during the 1960s. These findings do not support Hypothesis 7. If the linear model were appropriate, investment dependence might have positive effects because it leads to transfers of health technology and greater access to health aid.

Hypothesis 8 states that equality of resource distribution improves life expectancy within a nation. Table 8 presents evidence which does not support Hypothesis 8, since the effects on life expectancy of the income share received by the bottom 40% of recipients were significant for neither LDCs nor MDCs during the 1970s nor for LDCs during the 1960s.

Hypothesis 9 says that state strength increases life expectancy. Table 9 reports results of regressing life expectancy on economic development and state strength for samples of LDCs and MDCs for the

Table 6

Effect of World System Involvement on Life Expectancy and Infant Mortality
Linear Model

Part A: Life Expectancy, Ten-Year Periods

Period	Sample	n	Life Expectancy at Beginning of Period	ln GNP per capita	Trade as a Percent of GDP	Constant
1950-1960	LDCs	17	.415 (.134) .503***	12.48 (3.95) .446***	.075 (.058) .186	5.23
"	MDCs	17	.563 (.159) .801***	-.571 (1.70)-.071	.024 (.026) .159	32.48
1960-1970	LDCs	29	.811 (.088) .880***	2.69 (2.83) .090	-.006 (.023)-.018	8.74
"	MDCs	21	.704 (.120) .936***	-.659 (.956)-.099	-.001 (.013)-.008	24.44
1970-1978	LDCs	31	.913 (.057) .968***	-.099 (1.69)-.004	.005 (.011) .021	8.32
"	MDCs	22	.644 (.126) .838***	.575 (1.10) .083	-.019 (.010)-.220**	26.03
			b (S.E.b) Beta	b (S.E.b) Beta	b (S.E.b) Beta	

Part B: Infant Mortality Rate, Ten-Year Periods

Period	Sample	n	Infant Mortality at Beginning of Period	ln GNP per capita	Trade as a Percent of GDP	Constant
1960-1970	LDCs	29	.569 (.077) .782***	-13.99 (12.76)-.107	-.201 (.126)-.139*	57.72
"	MDCs	21	.860 (.061)1.15 ***	8.22 (3.17) .204***	.037 (.031) .063	-31.35
1970- 1977/80	LDCs	23	.579 (.232) .524***	-17.65 (24.09)-.139	-.109 (.178)-.125	66.28
	MDCs	22	.605 (.056) .980***	.006 (2.91) .0002	.008 (.021) .021	-.01
			b (S.E.b) Beta	b (S.E.b) Beta	b (S.E.b) Beta	

$* \ p < .10$
$** \ p < .05$
$*** \ p < .01$

Table 7

Effect of Investment Dependence on Life Expectancy
Linear Model

Period	Sample	n	Life Expectancy at Beginning of Period	ln GNP per capita	Investment Dependence per capita	Constant
1950-1960	LDCs	23	.800 (.104) .736***	10.64 (3.12) .363***	-.418 (1.08)-.039	-8.09
"	MDCs	22	.579 (.119) .926***	-.099 (1.68)-.011	-.430 (.472)-.136	30.36
1960-1970	LDCs	45	.849 (.073) .864***	4.23 (2.83) .132*	-.344 (.734)-.026	1.98
"	MDCs	23	.769 (.091) .964***	-1.31 (1.10)-.164	.646 (.494) .150	22.42
			b (S.E.b) Beta	b (S.E.b) Beta	b (S.E.b) Beta	

* $p < .10$
*** $p < .01$

Table 8

Effect of Income Equality on Life Expectancy
Linear Model

Period	Sample	n	Life Expectancy at Beginning of Period	ln GNP per capita	Income Share of Bottom 40% of Recipients	Constant
1960-1970	LDCs	27	.923 (.070) .957***	.066 (2.68) .002	-.126 (.147)-.047	10.37
1970-1978	LDCs	37	.892 (.064) .938***	1.13 (2.04) .040	.023 (.122) .010	6.01
"	MDCs	19	.671 (.160) .836***	-.792 (1.63)-.097	-.059 (.061)-.148	28.79
			b (S.E.b) Beta	b (S.E.b) Beta	b (S.E.b) Beta	

*** $p < .01$

Table 9

Effect of State Strength on Life Expectancy
Linear Model

Period	Sample	n	Life Expectancy at Beginning of Period	Index of Economic Development	Government Revenue per capita	Constant
1910-1930	LDCs	8	1.47 (.413) .865**	-1.05 (1.69)-.141	.003 (.017) .044	-9.06
"	MDCs	15	.973 (.141)1.03 ***	.289 (.660) .052	-.007 (.007)-.146	9.68
1930-1950	LDCs	14	.557 (.202) .638***	-1.03 (1.30)-.188	.019 (.019) .231	24.64
"	MDCs	23	.549 (.097) .813***	.204 (1.02) .029	-.001 (.001)-.102	35.12
1950-1970	LDCs	24	.778 (.157) .713***	2.69 (1.25) .273**	.002 (.004) .068	22.17
"	MDCs	22	.444 (.071) .871***	-.109 (.269)-.054	-.0003(.0004)-.120	41.98
			b (S.E.b) Beta	b (S.E.b) Beta	b (S.E.b) Beta	

** p < .05
*** p < .01

Table 10

Effect of Development, Health Care, and Equality on Life Expectancy

Linear Model

Period	Sample	n	Life Expectancy at Beginning of Period	ln GNP per capita	Physicians per 10,000 Population	Income Share of Bottom 40%	Constant
1960-1970	LDCs	26	.924 (.060) .965***	.810 (2.74) .024	-.030 (.147) -.014	-.078 (.136) -.029	7.74
1970-1978	LDCs	37	.889 (.067) .935***	.863 (2.58) .031	.035 (.200) .014	.015 (.132) .006	6.80
"	MDCs	18	.669 (.138) .830***	.695 (1.51) .084	-.290 (.108) -.466***	.081 (.074) .202	25.61
			b (S.E.b) Beta	b (S.E.b) Beta	b (S.E.b) Beta	b (S.E.b) Beta	

*** p < .01

periods 1910-1930, 1930-1950, and 1950-1970. State strength was never statistically significant, though its effects on life expectancy were positive for all three periods in LDCs and negative for all three periods in MDCs. The results for LDCs give slight support to Hypothesis 9.

It was decided to perform a rudimentary test of the assumption that resource distribution and economic development have recently become more important than health care in reducing mortality. Life expectancy in 1970 was regressed on 1960 levels of life expectancy, economic development, health care, and income equality for LDCs. For both LDCs and MDCs, 1978 life expectancy was regressed on 1970 levels of life expectancy, economic development, health care, and income equality. Results are summarized in Table 10. Most effects are not statistically significant and do not support the stated assumptions.

B. SUMMARY

The results of using a linear panel analysis model to assess the accuracy of Hypotheses 1 through 4 and 7 through 9 are mixed. Some findings for the effects of various factors on life expectancy may be interpreted to support those hypotheses, but few effects are statistically significant, and often signs are wrong. The two analyses in which infant mortality rate was the dependent variable are supportive of Hypotheses 3 and 4. The linear model may be adequate for analyses of changes in that particular measure of mortality, especially over short time periods. It is likely that the linear model is inappropriate to describe changes in life expectancy because that process is nonlinear. Chapter 8 describes a nonlinear model. It includes descriptions of results of use of that model in performance of additional analyses exploring factors contributing to mortality reduction. Its application yields results more supportive of theoretically predicted relationships than does the linear model discussed in this chapter.

Notes

1. As stated earlier (page 47), supply of physicians and amount of health aid can reflect earlier high mortality levels. This could explain the finding of significant negative effects on life expectancy.

Chapter 8

RESULTS FROM USE OF NONLINEAR MODEL

As stated in Chapter 5, trends in mortality over time are nonlinear. There is a limit to human longevity, and the rate of improvement in life expectancy slows as a population approaches the ceiling life expectancy possible under current conditions. Ultimately, the ceiling is life span, the maximum age that human beings could achieve under optimum conditions. There is no known exact figure for human life span, though it is generally assumed to be about 100 years, and may be an inborn physiological limit which has not changed in historical times. An interesting feature of the model described in this chapter is that if completely specified, it allows estimation of life span by two methods. See Appendix B for details.

The life expectancy of a population close to its longevity ceiling cannot grow so fast as that of populations farther from the ceiling. This nonlinear rate of increase in life expectancy is illustrated in Figures 2, 3A, 3B, 4A, 4B, 5A and 5B. A model of variables affecting life expectancy should reflect this nonlinearity. Because rate of change in life expectancy can be assumed to be relatively constant over short time periods, such a model can be used to examine changes over the ten and twenty year lag periods discussed in Chapters 5 and 7. An appropriate nonlinear model was developed.

A. NONLINEAR MODEL

If e^* represents the ceiling level of life expectancy and e_{t1} and e_{t2} represent, respectively, actual life expectancy at one point in time, t1, and at some later point in time, t2, then improvement in life expectancy from t1 to t2 depends on a comparison between e^* and e_{t1} :

$$e_{t2} - e_{tl} = \alpha (e^* - e_{tl}) \qquad\qquad [2]$$

where α represents the rate of approach of actual life expectancy to its ceiling and is a function of some factor or factors (X's) influencing change in the difference between ceiling and actual life expectancies:

$$\alpha = f (X_1 , \ldots X_n) \qquad\qquad [3]$$

For any specific time interval and given levels of X's in a particular population, α may be relatively constant so that [3] may be expressed as a linear relationship:

$$\alpha = \beta_0 + \beta_1 X_1 + \beta_2 X_2 + \ldots + \beta_n X_n \qquad\qquad [4]$$

By substituting [4] into [2], limiting to one the number of X's (independent variables influencing life expectancy), we obtain:

$$e_{t2} - e_{tl} = (\beta_0 + \beta_1 X)(e^* - e_{tl}) \qquad\qquad [5]$$

or

$$e_{t2} = \beta_0 e^* + (1 - \beta_0) e_{tl} + \beta_1 e^* X - \beta_1 e_{tl} X \qquad\qquad [6]$$

This can be rewritten as a linear equation, with the lagged value of the dependent variable on the right hand side:

$$e_{t2} = b_0 + b_1 e_{tl} + b_2 X + b_3 e_{tl} X \qquad\qquad [7]$$

where

$b_0 = \beta_0 e*$ the effect of the constant,

$b_1 = 1 - \beta_0$ the effect of the lagged dependent variable, e_{tl}

$b_2 = \beta_1 e*$ the effect of an independent variable, X, and

$b_3 = -\beta_1$ the effect of the interaction between e_{tl} and X.

The unstandardized regression coefficients (b's) obtained by estimating [7] can be used to solve for the β's in [6]. Comparisons of results from this nonlinear model with the results obtained using the linear model (discussed in Chapter 7) follow.

B. RESULTS

Tables 11 through 18 present results from use of the nonlinear model [5]. Generally, effects are not statistically significant because of small sample sizes, and the results are often fairly similar to those from the nonlinear model [1]. However, because life expectancy trends have been nonlinear, results from nonlinear model are a better test of the shifts in factors influencing life expectancy assumed in the literature.

Table 11 shows the effects of economic development alone on life expectancy. Economic development had uniformly positive, usually statistically significant effects on life expectancy in LDCs from 1890-1970. The only negative effects in LDCs were for the period 1970-1978. Effects of development in MDCs were mixed except for the period 1930-1950, when its effects were negative in all five relevant analyses reported in this chapter. The effects from this model are more consistently positive than those from the linear model. This finding supports Hypothesis 1.

Table 11

Effect of Economic Development on Life Expectancy
Nonlinear Model

Period	Sample	n	Constant	Index of Economic Development
1890–1910	LDCs	5	.120	.081
"	MDCs	5	-.640	.421
1910–1930	LDCs	8	.312	1.53 *
"	MDCs	15	.176	-.143
1930–1950	LDCs	14	1.11	.512
"	MDCs	27	.554	-.225
1950–1970	LDCs	25	.383	.399*
"	MDCs	23	.512	.104

* $p < .10$

Table 12

Effect of Health Care Availability on Life Expectancy
Nonlinear Model

Part A: Twenty-Year Periods

Period	Sample	n	Constant	Index of Economic Development	Physicians per 10,000 Population
1930–1950	MDCs	16	.180**	−.424	.083
1950–1970	LDCs	25	.336***	.575***	.096***
"	MDCs	16	.324***	.334*	−.006

Part B: Ten-Year Periods

Periods	Sample	n	Constant	ln GNP per capita	Physicians per 10,000 Population
1950/55– 1960/65	LDCs	56	−.480***	.191***	.009
	MDCs	30	.367	−.058	.020
1960/65– 1970/75	LDCs	56	−.080***	.037	.013**
	MDCs	30	.392	−.105	.005
1970/75– 1978	LDCs	56	−.060***	.054	.008
	MDCs	30	−1.29 ***	.680**	−.066**

* $p < .10$ ** $p < .05$ *** $p < .01$

Table 12 presents evidence of the effects of health care availability on life expectancy. In this and all subsequent analyses, economic development level was included in the equation as a control. In LDCs, health care had consistently positive effects, and it had positive effects in MDCs until after 1950. These results are clearly more supportive of Hypothesis 2 than those from use of ordinary linear panel analysis. The recent negative effects in MDCs are possible evidence of the diminishing returns effect of conventional medicine on life expectancy suggested in Chapter 7.

The evidence presented in Table 13 does not support Hypothesis 3. The results from estimating the nonlinear model, like those from linear panel analysis presented in Table 5, show that the only significant effects for international health aid are recent negative ones in MDCs. This probably results from aid being directed to the poorest countries, which have the shortest life expectancies. Though public health programs introduced from outside have undoubtedly influenced cause-specific death rates, these results do not demonstrate their impact.

Table 14 presents mixed results regarding effects of world system involvement on life expectancy. For LDCs, trade as a percent of GDP had a significant positive effect for 1950-1960 and a significant negative effect for 1960-1970. The former result supports Hypothesis 4, but the latter does not. Effects for MDCs were negative, but insignificant. World system involvement as measured by trade may have become a less important indicator of spreading world system values and technology. Other measures of this concept might yield different results. However, most of the effect of world system involvement may be measurable only indirectly, through economic development and health care. Generally, the results presented in Table 14 resemble those from the linear model (Table 6).

The linear model did not support Hypothesis 7. Table 15 presents results which do show negative effects of investment dependence on life expectancy in LDCs and support Hypothesis 7. Dependence had a significant negative effect in LDCs from 1950-1960 and an insignificant negative effect in a larger sample of LDCs from 1960-1970. As was the case with the linear model, dependence had a positive effect in MDCs for 1960-1970. Perhaps the dependent MDCs are more likely to receive technologies and health aid from the nations on which they depend than are dependent LDCs. The contacts between developed

Table 13

Effect of International Health Aid on Life Expectancy
Nonlinear Model

Part A: Twenty-Year Periods

Period	Sample	n	Constant	Index of Economic Development	Rockefeller Found. Aid per 1000 pop.
1910–1930	LDCs	8	.993	1.16	−.105
"	MDCs	15	.175***	−.182	.027
1930–1950	LDCs	14	1.47	.583	−.178
"	MDCs	27	.551***	−.208	−.001

Period	Sample	n	Constant	Index of Economic Development	WHO Aid per 1000 pop.
1950–1970	LDCs	24	.302***	.341*	−.005
"	MDCs	25	.667***	−.072	−.044***

Part B: Ten-Year Periods

Period	Sample	n	Constant	ln GNP per capita	WHO Aid per 1000 pop.
1950–1960	LDCs	23	−1.55 ***	.805***	−.014
"	MDCs	22	.401	−.053	.006
1960–1970	LDCs	43	−.450***	.271***	−.001
"	MDCs	26	−.360*	.294	−.049
1970–1978	LDCs	76	.278***	−.016	−.001
"	MDCs	30	.264	.030	−.044

* p < .10   ** p < .05   *** p < .01

Table 14

Effect of World System Involvement on Life Expectancy
Nonlinear Model

Part A: Twenty-Year Periods

Period	Sample	n	Constant	Index of Economic Development	Trade as a Percent of GDP
1910–1930	MDCs	14	.001***	.079	.220
1930–1950	MDCs	24	.836	-.438***	-.414
1950–1970	LDCs	17	.740	.587*	-.586
"	MDCs	14	.691***	.268	.247

Part B: Ten-Year Periods

Period	Sample	n	Constant	ln GNP per capita	Trade as a Percent of GDP
1950–1960	LDCs	17	-1.74 **	.751	.012*
"	MDCs	17	-.020	.242	-.004
1960–1970	LDCs	29	-.070***	.262	-.009***
"	MDCs	21	.726	-.051	-.006
1970–1978	LDCs	31	-.210***	.105	.001
"	MDCs	22	-.740*	.351	-.001

* p < .10   ** p < .05   *** p < .01

Table 15

Effect of Investment Dependence on Life Expectancy
Nonlinear Model

Period	Sample	n	Constant	ln GNP per capita	Investment Dependence per capita
1950-1960	LDCs	23	-3.01 ***	1.14 ***	-.350***
"	MDCs	22	-.080	.147	-.057
1960-1970	LDCs	45	-.640***	.345***	-.009
"	MDCs	23	1.31	-.169	.487***

*** p < .01

core nations and developed dependent ones (semi-peripheral MDCs) may be more intense and comprehensive than those between MDCs and the peripheral LDCs which depend on them. This tends to support predictions derived from dependency theory. Additional analyses covering more time periods should prove fruitful in the future.

Adelman (1963), Preston (1978b), and Schultz (1976) suggest an increasing role for resource distribution in longevity gains as effects of other factors yield diminishing returns. Table 16 presents results of analyses of the effects of income equality on life expectancy in LDCs for 1960-1970 and 1970-1978 and in MDCs for 1970-1978. The only statistically significant effect is for MDCs, and it is negative. Neither these results nor those presented in Table 8 support Hypothesis 8. In fact, income equality had a positive effect from 1960-1970 and a negative one from 1970-1978 in LDCs, tending to refute the pattern of time trends hypothesized in the literature. Either the patterns hypothesized in the literature are incorrect or the measure of equality is faulty, or both. Perhaps more time is required for resource distribution to show the expected effects. We would be better able to assess its effects with improved measures of income equality available over time for more countries.

The effects of state strength, which Hypothesis 9 says should increase life expectancy, are presented in Table 17. The results are not statistically significant, except in LDCs from 1950-1970, when government revenue per capita had a slightly significant positive effect (p < .25). This provides some support for Hypothesis 9. More sensitive measures are needed for earlier times to test this application of world system theory.

C. COMBINED EFFECTS OF DEVELOPMENT, HEALTH CARE AND INEQUALITY

It has been asserted that economic development had its greatest influence on mortality before 1910 in MDCs and before 1930 and after 1960 in LDCs (Arriaga and Davis 1969; Schultz 1976). Health technology is assumed to have been more important than economic development in increasing life expectancy in LDCs and MDCs from 1930-1950

Table 16

Effect of Income Equality on Life Expectancy
Nonlinear Model

Period	Sample	n	Constant	ln GNP per capita	Income Share of Bottom 40%
1960-1970	LDCs	27	-1.00 ***	.390**	.015
1970-1978	LDCs	37	.589	-.137	-.012
"	MDCs	19	3.08	-.308	-.107***

** p < .05   *** p < .01

Table 17

Effect of State Strength on Life Expectancy
Nonlinear Model

Period	Sample	n	Constant	Index of Economic Development	Government Revenue per capita
1910-1930	LDCs	8	.358	1.65	.003
"	MDCs	15	-.030***	-.059	.001
1930-1950	LDCs	14	2.00	.913**	-.004
"	MDCs	23	.400***	-.302	.001
1950-1970	LDCs	24	.394***	.535***	.001
"	MDCs	22	.626***	.057	-.0001

** $p < .05$ *** $p < .01$

Table 18

Effect of Development, Health Care, and Equality on Life Expectancy
Nonlinear Model

Period	Sample	n	Constant	ln GNP per capita	Physicians per 10,000 Population	Income Share of Bottom 40%	r^2
1960-1970	LDCs	26	-.920***	.331**	.023*	.020**	.98
1970-1978	LDCs	37	1.28	-.390*	.045*	-.022*	.94
"	MDCs	18	2.93	-.530	.064	-.101	.85

* p < .10   ** p < .05   *** p < .01

(Adelman 1963; Arriaga 1970a and b; Arriaga and Davis 1969; Davis 1956; Preston 1976 and 1978b; Schultz 1976; Stolnitz 1965). It has been argued that in the 1950s, diffusion of health technology and medicine had diminishing effects on life expectancy, to be replaced in importance by economic development and resource distribution in LDCs (Adelman 1963; Schultz 1976).

Table 18 presents results of simultaneously comparing the effects of economic development, health care availability, and income equality on life expectancy in LDCs from 1960-1970 and 1970-1978 and in MDCs from 1970-1978. These results do not support an assumption that economic development and resource distribution have recently become more important than health care in extending longevity. In LDCs, the effects of economic development and income equality shifted from significantly positive for 1960-1970 to significantly negative for 1970-1978. The effect of health care was significantly positive during both periods. This analysis indicates that the shifts in relative influence of these variables on life expectancy expected by Accinelli and Mueller (1980), Adelman (1963), and Schultz (1976) have not yet occurred. This analysis does not support Preston's (1978b) belief that since the late 1960s, health care has become less important and economic development has become more important in reducing mortality in LDCs.

D. SUMMARY AND DISCUSSION

These analyses of the effects of economic development, health care availability, international health aid, world system involvement, investment dependence, income equality, and state strength on life expectancy do not consistently support hypotheses which were derived from the demographic literature. Neither do they support the timing of shifts in the relative importance of variables which are suggested in the literature and summarized in Table 1. However, they do indicate *some* of the expected effects and some interesting shifts in the impact of the variables on mortality. Distinctions between LDCs' and MDCs' processes of mortality reduction over time are clarified.

Some of the effects reported in this chapter are summarized in Table 19. A plus or minus sign represents a statistically significant

Table 19

Summary of Findings from Analyses Using the Nonlinear Model
Effects of Independent Variables on Life Expectancy

LDCs:	1890-1910	1910-1930	1930-1950	1950-1970	1950-1960	1960-1970	1970-1978
Development	(+)	+	+	+	+	+	-(+)
Health Care				+	(+)	+	+
Health Aid		(-)	(-)	(-)	(-)	(-)	(-)
World System				(-)	+	-	(+)
Inv. Dependence					-	(-)	
Income Equality						+	
State Strength			(+)	(-)	(+)		

MDCs:	1890-1910	1910-1930	1930-1950	1950-1970	1950-1960	1960-1970	1970-1978
Development	(+)	(+ -)	-	+(-)	(+ -)	(+ -)	+(-)
Health Care			(+)	(-)	(+)	(+)	-(+)
Health Aid		(+)	(-)	-	(+)	(-)	(-)
World System		(+)	(-)	(+)	(-)	(-)	(-)
Inv. Dependence					(-)	+	
Income Equality							-
State Strength		)	(+)	(-)			

```
    +   significant positive effects
    -   significant negative effects
   (+)  nonsignificant positive effects
   (-)  nonsignificant negative effects
  (+ -) nonsignificant positive and negative effects
```

positive or negative effect (found in one or more of the analyses based on the nonlinear model) of a variable on life expectancy at birth. A plus or minus sign in parentheses represents a positive or negative effect which was not statistically significant, but was found in one or more analyses.

Among the noteworthy effects over time of variables on life expectancy discussed earlier in this chapter and summarized in Table 19 are:

1. *Development* (Economic Development): In LDCs, consistently positive effects until the 1970s, when there were some significant negative effects. In MDCs, effects were positive in some analyses, negative in others.

2. *Health Care*: In LDCs, consistently positive effect since 1950. In MDCs, some significant negative effects in the 1970s.

3. *Health Aid* (International Health Aid): In LDCs, consistently negative effects since 1910. In MDCs, negative effects in recent decades.

4. *Inv. Dependence* (Investment Dependence): In LDCs, negative effects, 1950-1970. In MDCs, positive effects, 1960-1970.

5. *Income Equality*: In LDCs, positive effects, 1960-1970 and negative effects, 1970-1978. In MDCs, negative effects, 1970-1978.

Neither world system involvement nor state strength had significant effects on life expectancy in the analyses reported here. Other empirical measures of these conceptual variables might yield more definitive results.

One of the most interesting results summarized in Table 19 is an apparent similarity between factors influencing life expectancy in LDCs, 1970-1978, and in MDCs, 1930-1950. In each case, economic development and international health aid had negative effects, and health care a positive one. Perhaps the similarity in patterns is mere coincidence; perhaps factors inherent in mortality reduction have produced them. When 1990 mortality data become available, separate analyses should be performed to disclose whether Latin American and Asian LDCs were indeed following patterns in the 1970s and 1980s similar to those prevailing in Western nations forty years earlier.

Examination of Figures 2, 3A, 3B, 5A and 5B suggests another similarity, between rates of improvement in life expectancy (slopes) in Latin American and Asian LDCs from 1970 to 1978 and in MDCs from 1930 to 1950. Life expectancy in MDCs (or Western nations) was about 60 years in 1930, and Latin American and Asian LDCs reached that level by about 1970. This suggests that a life expectancy of approximately 60 years represents a threshold after which medical inputs in addition to public health have an enhanced ability to extend longevity. The figures and nonlinear analyses support the idea of such a threshold. Though this possibility is not what others (Adelman 1963; Preston 1978b; Schultz 1976) have hypothesized, it merits additional study.

Chapter 9

CONCLUSIONS

A. SUMMARY OF FINDINGS

This work has extended mortality research in several ways. The emphasis on convergence of life expectancies in LDCs and MDCs over the last century is significant. Use of a theoretical framework to explain these trends is new. Panel analysis and the nonlinear model are methodological improvements over previous work. The analyses reported here suggest basic weaknesses in a number of the models, methods, and conclusions arrived at by other researchers.

The most important result is a clear, graphic representation of strikingly different nonlinear processes of rising life expectancies in LDCs and MDCs and in different regions of the world (Chapter 6). Convergence of life expectancy levels of geographical regions and types of countries is marked, but there is evidence of convergence slowing or stopping, as well as possibly different ceilings for subgroups of LDCs and MDCs.

The results described in Chapter 8 give some support to theoretical assumptions about comparative impacts on life expectancy of economic development, health care availability, international health aid, world system involvement, investment dependence, income equality, and state strength. It becomes clear that use of theory to explain mortality trends can be productive. Among the theoretically relevant findings

101

are that economic development has until recently been very important
to mortality reduction in LDCs, but has varied in importance to MDCs.
Health aid appears to have had no positive impact, possibly because it
is directed to poorer nations in response to already appalling mortality
levels. Investment dependence hinders mortality reduction in LDCs,
but probably not in MDCs. Income equality produces mixed effects,
not the positive ones predicted by theory. Complexity of these effects
suggests that the processes of demographic transition and economic
development are indeed as varied and idiosyncratic as scholars increasingly suggest.

The analytical methods introduced here (panel regression and use of
a nonlinear model) have the potential to provide clearer answers about
comparative influence of factors over time on life expectancy. Because
life expectancy trends unquestionably have been nonlinear, results from
the nonlinear model discussed in Chapter 8 are a better test of the
shifts in effects of variables assumed in the literature than are results
from the linear model discussed in Chapter 7.

B. RECOMMENDATIONS FOR RESEARCH

Problems associated with these analyses included small samples,
insufficient data, poor data quality, and multicollinearity. Future
research should emphasize increasing sample sizes through
interpolating and extrapolating data. When data become available for
large numbers of nations, there can be more focus on the period since
1950. When available, life expectancy data for 1990 (and after) will add
much to the analysis involving recent decades. Various additional
measures could be used to examine effects of state strength, world system involvement, dependency, and access to health care. Health care
measures which differentiate between public health and personal
hygiene should be used. Contrasts should be drawn between factors influencing mortality in the West, Latin America, Asia, and Africa and
between "old" and "new" nations (distinguished by length of
independence, type of dependency, and stage in the mortality
transition) to discover other possible types of variation in mortality reduction processes.

Methods could be improved by using the pooled cross-sections and time-series analysis method recommended by Stolnitz (1981) and used, in part, by Gravelle and Backhouse (1987) in investigating 1977 infant and perinatal mortality in a small sample of MDCs. This method is superior to separate panel analyses for each time period because it increases the sample size by using all the data simultaneously. It allows testing of the assumption that the causal structure remains constant over time.[1]   It also deals with problems of autocorrelation of disturbances from one time period to the next (Hannan and Young 1977).[2] Other nonlinear models incorporating a time element should be developed.   Robust regression methods could be applied to minimize the impact of multicollinearity of independent variables and interaction terms in nonlinear models like the one in Chapter 8.

Mortality research should continue to be linked with various social science theories.   Results should suggest directions for further research. This can increase the usefulness of empirical work in development planning. Above all, future research should employ theory and improved methodologies to explain mortality differences within and across nations.

Notes

1. This assumption can be tested by comparing the results from pooled waves of data with and without a dummy variable for year. If effects are different for the independent variable with and without the dummy, causal processes probably are not constant.

2. Panel models like the one used in Chapter 7 can result in ordinary least squares (OLS) estimators which are both biased and inconsistent if the disturbances are autocorrelated, because important causal variables are omitted from the model and there is non-independence of observations. Use of OLS when there are autocorrelated disturbances biases standard errors toward zero and yields inflated levels of statistical significance (Hannan 1979). Pooled cross-sections and time-series analysis can correct for this autocorrelation bias, if several waves of data are available for the same group of nations (Hannan and Young 1977). This method employs modified least squares rather than OLS to avoid biased and inconsistent estimators.

Chapter 10

POLICY IMPLICATIONS

Policy makers should note that this analysis suggests life expectancy in LDCs may still be substantially extended by increasing medical services (including physicians, dentists, nurses, hospitals, and clinics) in addition to implementing simple public health measures designed to reduce infectious and epidemic diseases. Improving medical services is expensive, but our analysis indicates that in LDCs only medical services have had consistently positive effects on life expectancy. Efforts to alter the effects of investment dependence in LDCs so that more ideas and technologies diffuse during economic interaction may also, as a side effect, help reduce mortality. It is in the interest of both LDCs and MDCs to expedite mortality reduction in the former because mortality reduction may speed fertility reduction, help slow population growth, and facilitate economic development.

Policy recommendations for LDCs and MDCs are somewhat different, though common concerns apply. The following sections summarize policy recommendations made by social scientists. It must be remembered, however, that mortality patterns are so varied that numerous possible paths may lead to further mortality reduction.

105

A. POLICIES FOR LDCs

Recommendations for mortality-reducing policies in LDCs are varied. Experts emphasize that further economic development is essential, but since foreign indebtedness of LDCs has increased dramatically in recent decades, the levels of economic growth which were once thought possible seem presently unattainable. Debt repayment limits the resources that can be devoted to capital investment in diverse economic enterprises, development of infrastructures, education, and applying public health measures. Economic dependency can impede development.

Successful implementation of health policies has, as Vallin and Lopez (1985) indicated, resulted in significant variation in mortality patterns. The range of life expectancy among LDCs is large. Furthermore, mortality reduction has aggravated inequalities within some LDCs, giving a few elites access to modern medical attention while many poorer people have not benefited from basic public health measures. Redistribution of income and reduction of inequalities within LDCs seems unlikely, given the political realities of instability, political corruption, lack of civic virtue, failure of commitment to democracy, and an all too human greediness in elites.

Sell and Kunitz (1986-7) recommended implementation of the same sort of social welfare programs which increased life expectancy in both MDCs of the core (Scandinavia) and LDCs of the periphery (Sri Lanka and Costa Rica). Caldwell (1986a), however, decided that Sri Lanka, Kerala, and Costa Rica achieved low mortality through measures other LDCs are unlikely to duplicate: substantial female autonomy, dedication to education, open political systems, minimal class structures, and histories of egalitarianism, radicalism, national consensus, and populism. These societies took for granted the idea that political and social energies should be devoted to social welfare programs. Whereas Sell and Kunitz proposed that multinational development assistance programs like the International Development Agency be strengthened,[1] Caldwell contended that LDCs need to adopt programs which will further female autonomy and develop efficient local health services.

Bell (1985) pointed out that there are mortality differences among countries at similar per capita income levels. These differences result from income distribution, education of mothers, allocation of health resources to prevention, public health, and community-based programs. Mortality reduction in LDCs, he argued, can be hastened by policies to encourage economic development and increase per capita income, to redistribute income while sustaining economic growth, encourage research into the special health problems of LDCs, encourage education, especially of women, and to emphasize public health, preventive actions, and paramedical personnel. "Political will" to implement change is needed to overcome the economic, social and political obstacles to change.[2] Vallin and Lopez (1985) pointed out that where governments have been committed to improved health, mortality reduction has been dramatic. They contrast India with China, Haiti with Cuba. China and Cuba have achieved rapid increases in life expectancy because their governments and people wished to do so.

For programs to have maximum impact, they should be appropriate and directed to the population with greatest need. As Antonovsky (1981) stated, investments in education and other social services may favor the middle and upper classes disproportionately. Such investment must be directed into programs which will benefit the lower classes. Policy experts have also emphasized the value of primary health care, which is accessible, affordable and acceptable (socially relevant) to the general population (Ruzicka and Hansluwka 1982; U.N. 1984). It is also frequently recommended that social services, especially education, be provided to women (Bell 1985; Caldwell 1986a).

Palloni (1985) recommended that Latin American governments endorse and be responsible for literacy campaigns. They should establish mechanisms to guarantee equality of access to basic goods and services, and invest to alter material conditions in some communities. Nutrition should be improved, as should sanitation and water supplies.

B. POLICIES FOR MDCs

International and intranational income differences become the major determinants of mortality after epidemic diseases are controlled, according to Mosk and Johannson (1986). At very high standards of living, when income differences within a society become less significant, then biological factors and culturally influenced or individual choice factors become the principal determinants of mortality. Most MDCs have achieved relatively high per capita income levels along with environmental control, reducing the impact of epidemic diseases.

Within MDCs, mortality inequalities persist because of socio-economic inequalities (based on ascribed statuses like ethnicity, race, religion, and sex or achieved statuses like education, or occupation) or life style factors like diet, exercise patterns, and drug use (primarily tobacco and alcohol, but sometimes other substances). On the one hand, there are those who enjoy good education, health care, and longevity. They have many choices and opportunities, including chances for life in the Weberian sense. On the other hand, there are those who have fewer choices and opportunities. Cultural patterns tend to lead these individuals to have lifestyles which preclude long, healthy, productive lives.[3] Relatively disadvantaged people are more likely to have unbalanced diets, to smoke, abuse alcohol, and suffer preventable degenerative diseases.

In the United States a disproportionate number of the disadvantaged are racial and ethnic minorities. Differences in infant mortality, deaths from accidents and crime, and incidence of many diseases (including AIDS) mark these people as disadvantaged. Unless these people adopt healthy lifestyles and society chooses to help alleviate problems, social bifurcation will become more pronounced. Although mortality reduction has helped diminish fatalism and given people a sense of personal efficacy (Preston 1977), not everyone has chosen to take advantage of increased life expectancy. Self-control is frequently weak and societal intervention often inadequate among those who make life-shortening choices.

According to Vallin (1981) and Antonovsky (1981), we cannot hope to eliminate inequality with respect to death without eliminating social inequality. Reduction of excess mortality (preventable deaths) among the poor requires a thorough transformation of the least privileged social categories rather than new therapies and medical facilities.

MDCs' mortality-related problems include those which result from age distribution of the population. Populations with large numbers and proportions of elderly people devote resources to provide pensions, housing, expensive medical procedures, and sometimes special nursing care. In turn, providing for needs of the elderly may cause under-investment in children's education, health, and care. Financing social programs in MDCs healthy economic growth. Even with economic growth an increasing tax burden will rest on each worker to support social services, because mortality and fertility reduction cause working-age populations to shrink or remain static (O.E.C.D. 1988). Citizens of MDCs will have to decide whether to improve social program benefits which require tax increases and increased social security contributions. Finally, MDCs face deciding whether the quality of life in old age is adequate and whether the costs associated with maintaining life are worth paying.

C. SUMMARY

Ironically, mortality reduction has resulted in a growing proportion of the world's population being from the lower classes and residing in LDCs. This condition occurred because mortality reduction often results in greatest gains for disadvantaged groups (Preston 1977). Also, fertility reduction typically occurred first in higher social classes and wealthier nations, and later (if at all) in poorer classes and nations. Further mortality reduction in LDCs will make the typical individual and country poorer, on average, unless mortality reduction is combined with effective fertility reduction.

Inequality is the most acute problem. Examination of mortality-related policy considerations for both LDCs and MDCs results in the conclusion that until social conditions and cultures are made more uniform, equality of life expectancy are not likely to be attained. Uneven distribution of values favoring wholesome lifestyles and unequal access to resources and opportunities pose overwhelming barriers to equality of life expectancy. If world humanitarian ideals are to be realized, chances for longer life must be distributed more evenly. The work of other investigators and the work reported here suggest ways in which this form of inequality, if not eliminated, can be reduced. If the life expectancy differentials within countries and between MDCs and LDCs persist, discord within and between societies will undoubtedly be exacerbated.

Notes

1. Sell and Kunitz concluded international development assistance programs like I.D.A. help reduced mortality because nations borrowing from those programs during the 1970s experienced life expectancy increases.

2. Bell also stated that increasing cigarette consumption in LDCs will produce increases in lung cancer in the future unless LDCs' health planners implement programs to discourage smoking and promote healthful diet and lifestyle.

3. Nam and Myers (1987) pointed out that it is sometimes useful to examine the small group and individual processes through which health is improved. Focus in policy formulation on the influence of agents of socialization can produce individual choices which are likely to increase longevity. Caldwell (1984) explained that frequently policy makers must attempt to convince people to *use* health services, particularly in LDCs, where modern medical procedures are traditionally distrusted. Programs which will convince agents of socialization (parents, religious authorities, and others) to use health services might sometimes be required, even in MDCs, to assure utilization of health-maximizing measures.

Appendix A

COMPOSITION OF SAMPLES

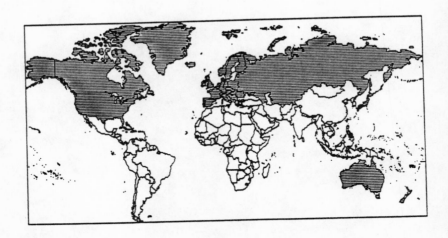

Figure 6. Location of MDCs ("West") used in samples for Figures 3A,
3B, 4A, 4B, 5A and regression analyses reported in Chapters 7 and 8.

(Figure was prepared using PC-GLOBE + (R), Comwell Systems, Inc.)

MORE DEVELOPED COUNTRIES ("WEST")

1870 - 1987   France, Sweden, United Kingdom

1890 - 1987   Australia, Belgium, France, Norway, Sweden, United Kingdom

1910 - 1987   Australia, Belgium, Denmark, Finland, France, Germany (West),[1] Iceland, Ireland, Japan, Luxembourg, Netherlands, New Zealand, Norway, Spain, Sweden, Switzerland, United Kingdom, United States

1930 - 1987   Australia, Belgium, Canada, Denmark, Finland, France, Germany (West), Greece, Iceland, Ireland, Italy, Japan, Luxembourg, Netherlands, New Zealand, Norway, Portugal, Spain, Sweden, Switzerland, United Kingdom, United States

1950 - 1987   Australia, Austria, Belgium, Canada, Denmark, Finland, France, Germany (West), Greece, Iceland, Ireland, Italy, Japan, Luxembourg, Netherlands, New Zealand, Norway, Portugal, Romania, Spain, Sweden, Switzerland, United Kingdom, United States, Yugoslavia

1970 - 1987   Australia, Austria, Belgium, Canada, Czechoslovakia, Denmark, Finland, France, Germany (East), Germany (West), Greece, Hungary, Iceland, Ireland, Italy, Japan, Luxembourg, Netherlands, New Zealand, Norway, Poland, Portugal, Romania, Scotland, Spain, Sweden, Switzerland, Union of Soviet Socialist Republics, United Kingdom, United States, Yugoslavia

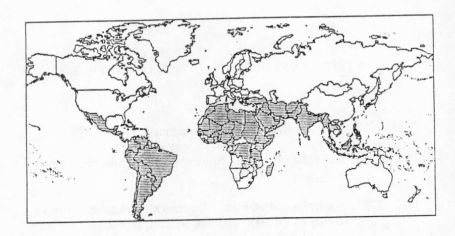

Figure 7. Location of LDCs used in samples for Figures 3A, 3B, 4A,
4B and regression analyses reported in Chapters 7 and 8.

(Figure was prepared using PC-GLOBE+(R), Comwell Systems, Inc.)

LESS DEVELOPED COUNTRIES (LDCs)

1890 - 1987 Brazil, Costa Rica, Guatemala, India, Mexico

1910 - 1987 Brazil, Chile, Colombia, Costa Rica, Guatemala, India, Mexico, Philippines, Sri Lanka, Trinidad and Tobago

1930 - 1987 Brazil, Chile, Colombia, Costa Rica, Guatemala, India, Mexico, Panama, Philippines, Sri Lanka, Taiwan, Thailand, Trinidad and Tobago, Turkey, Venezuela

1950 - 1987 Argentina, Brazil, Chile, Colombia, Costa Rica, Ecuador, Guatemala, Haiti, India, Iran, Israel, Ivory Coast, Jamaica, Korea (South), Malawi, Malaysia, Mauritius, Mexico, Panama, Peru, Philippines, Senegal, Singapore, Sri Lanka, Taiwan, Tanzania, Thailand, Trinidad and Tobago, Turkey, Venezuela, Zaire, Zambia

1970 - 1987 Afghanistan, Algeria, Argentina, Benin, Bolivia, Brazil, Burkina Faso, Burma, Burundi, Cameroon, Chad, Chile, Colombia, Costa Rica, Cuba, Ecuador, Egypt, El Salvador, Ethiopia, Ghana, Guatemala, Haiti, Honduras, Hong Kong, India, Indonesia, Iran, Iraq, Israel, Ivory Coast, Jamaica, Jordan, Kenya, Korea (South), Kuwait, Lebanon, Lesotho, Liberia, Libya, Madagascar, Malawi, Malaysia, Mali, Mauritania, Mauritius, Mexico, Morocco, Nepal, Nicaragua, Niger, Nigeria, Pakistan, Panama, Paraguay, Peru, Philippines, Rwanda, Saudi Arabia, Senegal, Sierra Leone, Singapore, Somalia, Sri Lanka, Sudan, Syria, Taiwan, Tanzania, Thailand, Togo, Trinidad and Tobago, Tunisia, Turkey, Uruguay, Venezuela, Yemen (South, People's Democratic Republic), Zaire, Zambia

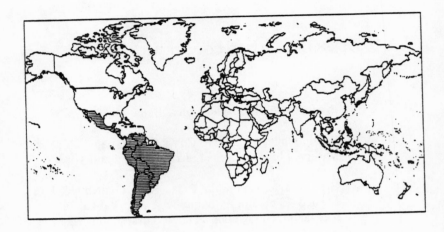

Figure 8. Location of Latin American countries used in samples for
Figure 5A and regression analyses reported in Chapters 7 and 8.

(Figure was prepared using PC-GLOBE + (R), Comwell Systems, Inc.)

LATIN AMERICAN COUNTRIES
(ALL LDCs)

1870 - 1987   Brazil, Costa Rica

1890 - 1987   Brazil, Costa Rica, Guatemala, Mexico

1910 - 1987   Brazil, Chile, Colombia, Costa Rica, Guatemala, Mexico, Trinidad and Tobago

1930 - 1987   Brazil, Chile, Colombia, Costa Rica, Guatemala, Mexico, Panama, Trinidad and Tobago, Venezuela

1950 - 1987   Argentina, Brazil, Chile, Colombia, Costa Rica, Ecuador, Guatemala, Haiti, Jamaica, Mexico, Panama, Peru, Trinidad and Tobago, Venezuela

1970 - 1987   Argentina, Bolivia, Brazil, Chile, Colombia, Costa Rica, Cuba, Ecuador, El Salvador, Guatemala, Haiti, Honduras, Jamaica, Mexico, Nicaragua, Panama, Paraguay, Peru, Trinidad and Tobago, Uruguay, Venezuela

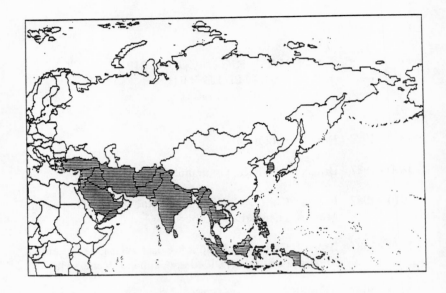

Figure 9. Location of Asian countries used in samples for Figure 5B
and regression analyses reported in Chapters 7 and 8.

(Figure was prepared using PC-GLOBE+(R), Comwell Systems, Inc.)

ASIAN COUNTRIES
(ALL LDCs)

1890 - 1987   India

1910 - 1987   India, Philippines, Sri Lanka

1930 - 1987   India, Philippines, Sri Lanka, Taiwan, Thailand, Turkey

1950 - 1987   India, Iran, Israel, Philippines, Korea (South), Malaysia, Singapore, Sri Lanka, Taiwan, Thailand, Turkey

1970 - 1987   Afghanistan,[2] Burma, Hong Kong, India, Indonesia, Iran, Iraq, Israel, Jordan, Korea (South), Kuwait, Lebanon,[3] Malaysia, Nepal, Pakistan, Philippines, Saudi Arabia, Singapore, Sri Lanka, Syria, Taiwan,[4] Thailand, Turkey, Yemen (South, People's Democratic Republic)

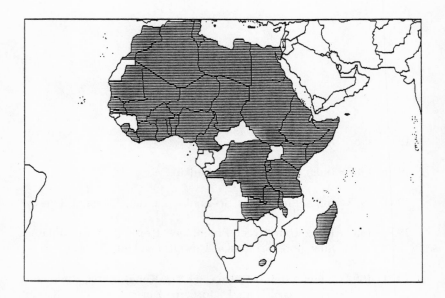

Figure 10. Location of African countries used in samples for Figure 5B
and regression analyses reported in Chapters 7 and 8.

(Figure was prepared using PC-GLOBE + (R), Comwell Systems, Inc.)

AFRICAN COUNTRIES
(ALL LDCs)

1950 - 1987   Ivory Coast, Malawi, Mauritius, Senegal, Tanzania, Zaire, Zambia

1970 - 1987   Algeria, Benin, Burkina Faso, Burundi, Cameroon, Chad, Egypt, Ethiopia, Ghana, Ivory Coast, Kenya, Lesotho, Liberia, Libya, Madagascar, Malawi, Mali, Mauritania, Mauritius, Morocco, Niger, Nigeria, Rwanda, Senegal, Sierra Leone, Somalia, Sudan, Tanzania, Togo, Tunisia, Zaire, Zambia

Notes

1. Since the division of Germany after World War II resulted in West Germany containing the vast majority of Germany's population and economic resources, data for 1910-1950 on Germany were attributed to West Germany. The constant German sample from 1910-1987 is called West Germany. From 1970-1987 East Germany was counted as a separate country.

2. No 1987 life expectancy data were available for Afghanistan from the I.B.R.D. because of the disruptions of Soviet invasion and civil war. Mean 1987 life expectancy for LDC and Asia samples were computed without Afghanistan.

3. No 1987 life expectancy data were available for Lebanon from the I.B.R.D. because of civil war. Mean 1987 life expectancy for LDC and Asia samples were computed without Lebanon.

4. No 1980 or 1987 life expectancy data were available for Taiwan from the I.B.R.D. because the People's Republic of China replaced Taiwan in the United Nations. Mean 1980 and 1987 life expectancy for LDC and Asia samples were computed without Taiwan.

Appendix B

LIFE SPAN ESTIMATES FROM THE NONLINEAR MODEL

The maximum age humans could reach under optimum conditions, e^*, can be estimated from the nonlinear model. Estimation of the b's in Equation 7 using regression analysis in Chapter 8 permits solving for the β's in Equation 6 and for e^*. The constant and lagged dependent variable are used to estimate e^* as follows:

$$\beta_0 = \frac{b_0}{e^*} \qquad \text{the effect of the constant or intercept}$$

$$\beta_0 = 1 - b_1 \qquad \text{the effect of the lagged dependent variable}$$

From these,

$$\frac{b_0}{e^*} = 1 - b_1$$

and

$$e^* = \frac{b_0}{\beta_0} = \frac{b_0}{(1 - b_1)}$$

The effects of independent variables and their interactions with the lagged dependent variable are used to estimate e^* as follows:

$$\beta_1 = \frac{b_2}{e^*} \qquad \text{the effect of } X_1, \text{ an independent variable}$$

$$\beta_1 = -b_3 \qquad \text{the effect of the interaction between } X_1 \text{ and the lagged dependent variable}$$

From these,

$$\frac{b_2}{e^*} = -b_3$$

and

$$b_2 = e^*(-b_3)$$

so

$$e^* = \frac{b_2}{(-b_3)}$$

Estimation of e^* from the regression analyses used to construct Table 18 yields the following results:

From the constant and the unstandardized regression coefficient for the lagged dependent variable:

e^* = 50.9   (LDCs, 1960-1970)

  = 54.5   (LDCs, 1970-1978)

  = 72.2   (MDCs, 1970-1978)

From the unstandardized regression coefficients for economic development and its interaction with the lagged dependent variable:

e^* = 55.1   (LDCs, 1960-1970)

  = 52.3   (LDCs, 1970-1978)

  = 71.0   (MDCs, 1970-1978)

From the standardized regression coefficients for health care availability and its interaction with the lagged dependent variable:

e^* = 78.3   (LDCs, 1960-1970)

  = 63.3   (LDCs, 1970-1978)

  = 67.7   (MDCs, 1970-1978)

From the unstandardized regression coefficients for income equality and its interaction with the lagged dependent variable:

$e^* =$ 51.0   (LDCs, 1960-1970)

$=$ 54.6   (LDCs, 1970-1978)

$=$ 70.5   (MDCs, 1970-1978)

These estimates of e^* are lower than the life span of about 100 years hypothesized for humans by experts. However, the model is not fully specified and if it were possible to include more independent variables in an analysis, e^* estimates might be higher. The above figures are encouraging, since they are within the realm of the possible and should be shorter than actual life span because not all factors influencing longevity were included in any version of the nonlinear model.

REFERENCES

Accinelli, M. Martha and Maria S. Mueller. 1980. "Why Argentina's Mortality is Rising." *Intercom* 8 (March): 8-9.

Adelman, Irma. 1963. "An Econometric Analysis of Population Growth." *American Economic Review* 53: 314-39.

Adelman, Irma and Cynthia Taft Morris. 1973. *Economic Growth and Social Equity in Developing Countries*. Stanford, California: Stanford University Press.

Ahluwalia, Montek S. 1974. "Income Inequality: Some Dimensions of the Problem." Pp. 3-37 in *Redistribution and Growth*, edited by H. Chenery, et al. London: Oxford University Press

Ahluwalia, Montek S. 1976. "Inequality, Poverty and Development." *Journal of Development Economics* 3: 307-42.

Antonovsky, Aaron. 1967. "Social Class, Life Expectancy, and Overall Mortality." *The Milbank Memorial Fund Quarterly* 45: 31-72.

Antonovsky, Aaron. 1981. "Implications of Socio-Economic Differentials in Mortality for the Health System." Pp. 42-52 in *Population Bulletin of the United Nations*, Number 13 (1980). New York: United Nations Department of International Economic and Social Affairs.

Arriaga, Eduardo E. 1968. *New Life Tables for Latin American Populations in the Nineteenth and Twentieth Centuries*. Berkeley, California: University of California.

129

Arriaga, Eduardo E. 1970a. *Mortality Decline and Its Demographic Effects in Latin America.* Berkeley, California: University of California.

Arriaga, Eduardo E. 1970b. "The Nature and Effects of Latin America's Non-Western Trend in Fertility." *Demography* 7: 483-501.

Arriaga, Eduardo E. 1981. "The Deceleration of the Decline of Mortality in LDCs: The Case of Latin America." Pp. 21-50 in *International Population Conference Manila 1981*, Vol. 2, International Union for the Scientific Study of Population (I.U.S.S.P.). Liège, Belgium: I.U.S.S.P.

Arriaga, Eduardo E. 1984. "Measuring and Explaining the Change in Life Expectancies." *Demography* 21: 83-96.

Arriaga, Eduardo E. and Kingsley Davis. 1969. "The Pattern of Mortality Change in Latin America." *Demography* 6: 223-42.

Azefor, M.N.A. 1981. "Counteracting Forces in the Continued Decline of Mortality in Africa." Pp. 5-20 in *International Population Conference Manila 1981*, Vol. 2, International Union for the Scientific Study of Population (I.U.S.S.P.). Liège, Belgium: I.U.S.S.P.

Behm, Hugo. 1979. "Socioeconomic Determinants of Mortality in Latin America." Pp. 140-65 in *Proceedings of the Meeting on Socioeconomic Determinants and Consequences of Mortality*, United Nations and World Health Organization. New York and Geneva: United Nations and World Health Organization.

Bell, David E. 1985. "What Policies Will Reduce Death Rates Most Rapidly in Less Developed Countries?" Pp. 493-505 in *Health Policy, Social Policy and Mortality Prospects* edited by Jacques Vallin and Alan D. Lopez. Liège, Belgium: Ordina Editions (I.N.E.D. and I.U.S.S.P.).

Boli-Bennett, John. 1976. *The Expansion of Nation-States, 1870-1970.* Stanford, California: Stanford University Ph.D. Dissertation.

Bourgeois-Pichat, Jean. 1985. "Recent Changes in Mortality in Industrialized Countries." Pp. 507-39 in *Health Policy, Social Policy and Mortality Prospects* edited by Jacques Vallin and Alan D. Lopez. Liège, Belgium: Ordina Editions (I.N.E.D. and I.U.S.S.P.).

Bradshaw, York W. 1988. "Reassessing Economic Dependency and Uneven Development: The Kenyan Experience." *American Sociological Review* 53: 693-708.

Caldwell, John C. 1984. "Introductory Remarks on Interactions between Health Mortality and Development." Pp. 106-11 in *Mortality and Health Policy: Proceedings of the Expert Group on Mortality and Health Policy,* Rome, 30 May to 3 June 1983. New York: United Nations Department of International Economic and Social Affairs.

Caldwell, John C. 1986a. "Routes to Low Mortality in Poor Countries." *Population and Development Review* 12: 171-220.

Caldwell, John C. 1986b. "The Role of Mortality Decline in Theories of Social and Demographic Transition." Pp. 31-42 in *Consequences of Mortality Trends and Differentials, Population Studies,* Number 95. New York: United Nations Department of International Economic and Social Affairs.

Chase-Dunn, Christopher. 1975. "The Effects of International Economic Dependence on Development and Inequality." *American Sociological Review* 40: 720-38.

Chisholm, Brock. 1967. "Contributions of Philanthropic Foundations to World Health." Pp. 346-52 in *U.S. Philanthropic Foundations,* edited by W. Weaver. New York: Harper and Row.

Cohen, Bernard P. 1980. *Developing Sociological Knowledge: Theory and Method.* Englewood Cliffs, New Jersey: Prentice-Hall.

Crimmins, Eileen M. 1981. "The Changing Pattern of American Mortality Decline." *Population and Development Review* 7: 229-54.

Davis, Kingsley. 1956. "The Amazing Decline of Mortality in Underdeveloped Areas." *American Sociological Review* 46: 305-18.

Davis, Kingsley and Judith Blake. 1956. "Social Structure and Fertility: An Analytic Framework." *Economic Development and Cultural Change* 4: 211-35.

Gaisie, S.K. 1981. "Some Aspects of Socio-Economic Determinants of Mortality in Tropical Africa." Pp. 16-25 in *Population Bulletin of the United Nations,* Number 13 (1980). New York: United Nations Department of International Economic and Social Affairs.

Gobalet, Jeanne G. and Larry J. Diamond. 1979. "Effects of Investment Dependence on Economic Growth." *International Studies Quarterly* 23: 412-44.

Gravelle, H.S.E. and Backhouse, M.E. 1987. "International Cross-Section Analysis of the Determination of Mortality." *Social Science and Medicine* 25: 427-41.

Grosse, Robert N. and Barbara H. Perry. 1982. "Correlates of Life Expectancy in Less Developed Countries." *Health Policy and Education* 2: 275-304.

Gwatkin, Davidson R. 1980. "Indications of Change in Developing Country Mortality Trends." *Population and Development Review* 6: 615-44.

Hannan, Michael T. 1979. "Methodological Overview." Pp. 17-33 in *National Economic Development and the World System*, edited by J.W. Meyer and M.T. Hannan. Chicago: University of Chicago Press.

Hannan, Michael T. and A. Young. 1977. "Estimation in Panel Models: Results on Pooling Cross-Sections and Time-Series." Pp. 52-83 in *Sociological Methodology*, edited by D. Heise. San Francisco, California: Jossey-Bass.

Hauser, Philip M. 1959. "Demographic Indicators of Economic Development." *Economic Development and Cultural Change* 7: 98-116.

Heiser, Victor. 1936. *An American Doctor's Odyssey*. New York: W.W. Norton.

Hoover, Greg A. 1989. "Intranational Inequality: A Cross-National Dataset." *Social Forces* 67: 1008-26.

Hout, Michael. 1980. "Trade Dependence and Fertility in Hispanic America; 1900-1975." Pp. 159-88 in *Studies of the Modern World-System*, edited by A. Bergesen. New York: Academic Press.

Inkeles, Alex and David H. Smith. 1974. *Becoming Modern*. Cambridge: Harvard University Press.

International Bank for Reconstruction and Development (I.B.R.D.) / World Bank). 1971. *World Tables*. Washington, D.C.: World Bank.

International Bank for Reconstruction and Development (I.B.R.D.) / World Bank). 1976. *World Tables*. Baltimore: Johns Hopkins University Press.

International Bank for Reconstruction and Development (I.B.R.D.) / World Bank). 1978 and 1979. *World Development Report*. Washington, D.C.: World Bank.

International Bank for Reconstruction and Development (I.B.R.D.) / World Bank). 1980, 1982 and 1989. *World Development Report*. New York: Oxford University Press.

International Monetary Fund (I.M.F.). 1950-1965. *Balance of Payments Handbook*. Volumes 8-18. Washington, D.C.: International Monetary Fund.

International Monetary Fund (I.M.F.). 1972. *International Financial Statistics 1972, Supplement*. Washington, D.C.: International Monetary Fund.

International Review Group of Social Science Research on Population and Development (I.R.G.). 1979. *Social Science Research for Population Policy: Directions for the 1980s*. Mexico City: International Review Group.

Jain, Shail. 1975. *Size Distribution of Income*. Washington, D.C.: World Bank.

Johansson, S. Ryan and Carl Mosk. 1987. "Exposure, Resistance and Life Expectancy: Disease and Death during the Economic Development of Japan, 1900-1960." *Population Studies* 41: 207-35.

Keyfitz, Nathan and Wilhelm Flieger. 1971. *Population: Facts and Methods of Demography*. San Francisco: W.H. Freeman.

King, Timothy. 1974. *Population Policies and Economic Development*. Baltimore: Johns Hopkins University Press.

Kunitz, Stephen J. 1983. "Speculations on the European Mortality Decline." *The Economic History Review* Second Series, Vol. 36: 349-64.

Kunitz, Stephen J. 1986. "Mortality Since Malthus." Pp. 279-302 in *The State of Population Theory*, edited by David Coleman and Roger Schofield. Oxford: Basil Blackwell Ltd.

Kuznets, Simon. 1955. "Economic Growth and Income Inequality." *American Economic Review* 45: 18-9.

Kuznets, Simon. 1980. "Recent Population Trends in Less Developed Countries and Implications for Internal Income Inequality." Pp. 471-511 in *Population and Economic Change in Developing Countries*, edited by R.A. Easterlin. Chicago: University of Chicago Press.

League of Nations (L.N.). 1924-1930. *International Health Yearbook*. Geneva: League of Nations.

Lenski, Gerhard E. 1966. *Power and Privilege*. New York: McGraw-Hill.

London, Bruce. 1988. "Dependence, Distorted Development, and Fertility Trends in Noncore Nations: A Structural Analysis of Cross-National Data." *American Sociological Review* 53: 606-18.

McDermott, Walsh. 1980. "Pharmaceuticals: Their Role in Developing Societies." *Science* 209: 240-45.

McKeown, Thomas. 1976. *The Modern Rise of Population*. New York: Academic Press.

Metropolitan Life Insurance Company. 1986. "Recent International Changes in Longevity." *Statistical Bulletin* 67(1): 16-21.

Meyer, John W. 1980. "The World Polity and the Authority of the Nation-State." Pp. 109-37 in *Studies of the Modern World System*, edited by A. Bergesen. New York: Academic Press.

Meyer, John W., John Boli-Bennett, and Christopher Chase-Dunn. 1975. "Convergence and Divergence in Development." Pp. 223-46 in *Annual Review of Sociology*, Vol. I, edited by A. Inkeles. Palo Alto, California: Annual Reviews.

Meyer, John W. and Michael T. Hannan, eds. 1979. *National Development and the World System*. Chicago: University of Chicago Press.

Mosk, Carl and S. Ryan Johansson. 1986. "Income and Mortality: Evidence from Modern Japan." *Population and Development Review* 12: 415-40.

Murray, Christopher J.L. 1987. "A Critical Review of International Mortality Data." *Social Science and Medicine* 25: 773-81.

Nam, Charles B. and George C. Myers. 1987. "Introduction: An Overview of Mortality Patterns and Their Policy Implications." *Population Research and Policy Review* 6: 97-104.

Nightingale, Elena. 1981. "Prospects for Reducing Mortality in Developed Countries by Changes in Day-to-Day Behavior." Pp. 207-29 in *International Population Conference Manila 1981*, Vol. 2, International Union for the Scientific Study of Population (I.U.S.S.P.). Liége, Belgium: I.U.S.S.P.

Oechsli, Frank Wm. and Dudley Kirk. 1975. "Modernization and the Demographic Transition in Latin America and the Caribbean." *Economic Development and Cultural Change* 23: 391-419.

Omran, Abdel R. 1971. "The Epidemiologic Transition: A Theory of the Epidemiology of Population Change." *The Milbank Memorial Fund Quarterly* 49 (4): 509-38.

Omran, Abdel R. 1983. "The Epidemiologic Transition Theory. A Preliminary Update." *Journal of Tropical Pediatrics* 29: 305-16.

Organisation for Economic Co-Operation and Development (O.E.C.D.). 1988. *Ageing Populations: The Social Policy Implications*. Paris: O.E.C.D.

Palloni, Alberto. 1981a. "Current Conditions of Mortality in Latin America with Emphasis on Infancy and Early Childhood." *Statistical Bulletin of the O.A.S.* 3(3-4): 1-26.

Palloni, Alberto. 1981b. "Mortality in Latin America: Emerging Patterns." *Population and Development Review* 7: 623-49.

Palloni, Alberto. 1985. "Health Conditions in Latin America and Policies for Mortality Change." Pp. 465-92 in *Health Policy, Social Policy and Mortality Prospects* edited by Jacques Vallin and Alan D. Lopez. Liége, Belgium: Ordina Editions (I.N.E.D. and I.U.S.S.P.).

Parks, Richard W. 1980. "Comment on Preston's 'Causes and Consequences of Mortality Decline in LDCs'." Pp. 352-3 in *Population and Economic Change in Developing Countries*, edited by R.A. Easterlin. Chicago: University of Chicago Press.

Pendleton, Brian F. and Shu-O. W. Yang. 1985. "Socioeconomic and Health Effects on Mortality Declines in Developing Countries." *Social Science and Medicine* 20: 453-60.

Pollard, J.H. 1988. "On the Decomposition of Changes in Expectation of Life and Differentials in Life Expectancy." *Demography* 25: 265-76.

Preston, Samuel H. 1975. "Health Programs and Population Growth." *Population and Development Review* 1: 189-99.

Preston, Samuel H. 1976. *Mortality Patterns in National Populations*. New York: Academic Press.

Preston, Samuel H. 1977. "Mortality Trends." Pp. 163-78 in *Annual Review of Sociology*, Vol. 3. Palo Alto, California: Annual Reviews, Inc.

Preston, Samuel H. 1978a. *The Effect of Infant and Child Mortality on Fertility*. New York: Academic Press.

Preston, Samuel H. 1978b. "Mortality, Morbidity, and Development." *Population Bulletin of the U.N. Economic Commission for Western Asia*, Number 15: 63-75.

Preston, Samuel H. 1980. "Causes and Consequences of Mortality Declines in LDCs During the Twentieth Century." Pp. 289-341 in *Population and Economic Change in Developing Countries*, edited by R.A. Easterlin. Chicago: University of Chicago Press.

Preston, Samuel H. 1986. "Mortality and Development Revisited." Pp. 34-40 in *Population Bulletin of the United Nations*, Number 18 (1985). New York: United Nations Department of International Economic and Social Affairs.

Preston, Samuel H. and Verne E. Nelson. 1974. "Structure and Change in Causes of Death: An International Summary." *Population Studies* 28: 19-51.

Rich, William. 1973. *Smaller Families Through Social and Economic Progress*. Washington, D.C.: Overseas Development Council.

Rockefeller Foundation (R.F.). 1923-1926, 1934-1942, and 1947-1950. *International Health Board* and *International Health Division Annual Reports*. New York: Rockefeller Foundation.

Rodgers, G.B. 1979. "Income and Inequality as Determinants of Mortality: An International Cross-Section Analysis." *Population Studies* 33: 343-51.

Rogers, Richard G. and Robert Hackenberg. 1987. "Extending Epidemiologic Transition Theory: A New Stage." *Social Biology* 34(3-4): 234-43.

Rogers, Richard G. and Sharon Wofford. 1989. "Life Expectancy in Less Developed Countries: Socioeconomic Development or Public Health?" *Journal of Biosocial Science* 21: 245-52.

Rokkan, Stein. 1975. "Dimensions of State Formation and Nation-Building." Pp. 562-600 in *The Formation of National States in Western Europe*, edited by C. Tilly. Princeton, New Jersey: Princeton University Press.

Rubinson, Richard. 1976. "The World-Economy and the Distribution of Income Within States: A Cross-National Study." *American Sociological Review* 41: 638-59.

Ruzicka, Lado T. 1984. "Intersectoral Aspects of Mortality Projections in Developing Countries." *World Health Statistics Quarterly* 37(3): 281-93.

Ruzicka, Lado T. and Harald Hansluwka. 1982. "Mortality Transition in South and East Asia: Technology Confronts Poverty." *Population and Development Review* 8: 567-88.

Sagan, L.A. and A.A. Afifi. 1978. *Health and Economic Development I: Infant Mortality*. Laxenburg, Austria: International Institute for Applied Systems Analysis.

Schoen, Robert. 1986. "The Role of Mortality Decline in Theories of Social and Demographic Transition." Pp. 20-30 in *Consequences of Mortality Trends and Differentials, Population Studies*, Number 95. New York: United Nations Department of International Economic and Social Affairs.

Schofield, Roger. 1984. "Population Growth in the Century after 1750: the Role of Mortality Decline." Pp. 17-39 in *Pre-Industrial Population Change*, edited by Tommy Bengtsson, Gunnar Fridizius, and Rolf Ohlsson. Stockholm: Almquist and Wiskell International.

Schultz, T. Paul. 1976. "Interrelationships Between Mortality and Fertility." Pp. 239-89 in *Population and Development*, edited by R.G. Ridker. Baltimore: Johns Hopkins University Press.

Scrimshaw, Susan. 1978. "Infant Mortality and Behavior in The Regulation of Family Size." *Population and Development Review* 4: 383-403.

Sell, Ralph R. and Stephen J. Kunitz. 1986-7. "The Debt Crisis and the End of an Era in Mortality Decline." *Studies in Comparative International Development* 21(4): 3-30.

Simon, Julian L. 1976. "Income, Wealth, and their Distribution as Policy Tools in Fertility Control." Pp. 36-76 in *Population and Development*, edited by R.G. Ridker. Baltimore: Johns Hopkins University Press.

Singer, H.W. 1976. "Income Distribution and Population Growth." Pp. 104-18 in *Population, Factor Movements, and Economic Development*, edited by H. Richards. Cardiff: University of Wales Press.

Stockwell, Edward G. 1960. "The Measurement of Economic Development." *Economic Development and Cultural Change* 8: 419-32.

Stockwell, Edward G. 1962. "Infant Mortality and Socio-Economic Status: A Changing Relationship." *The Milbank Memorial Fund Quarterly* 40: 101-19.

Stolnitz, George J. 1955. "A Century of International Mortality Trends: I." *Population Studies* 9: 24-55.

Stolnitz, George J. 1956. "A Century of International Mortality Trends: II." *Population Studies* 10: 17-42.

Stolnitz, George J. 1965. "Recent Mortality Trends in Latin America, Asia, and Africa." *Population Studies* 19: 117-38.

Stolnitz, George J. 1981. "Review of U.N. and W.H.O., *Proceedings of the Meeting on Socioeconomic Determinants and Consequences of Mortality, 1979*." *Population and Development Review* 7: 693-701.

Sundbarg, Gustav. 1968. *Apercus Statistiques Internationaux 1908*. New York: Gordon and Breach Science Publishers.

Tilly, Charles. 1975. *The Formation of National States in Western Europe*. Princeton, New Jersey: Princeton University Press.

United Nations (U.N.). 1953 and 1973. *The Determinants and Consequences of Population Trends*. New York: United Nations.

United Nations (U.N.). 1979 and 1980. *World Population Trends and Policies Monitoring Report*, Vol. I. New York: United Nations Department of Economic and Social Affairs.

United Nations (U.N.). 1981. *Population and Vital Statistics Report*, Series A, Vol. 33, Number 1. New York: United Nations.

United Nations (U.N.). 1982. *Levels and Trends of Mortality since 1950: A Joint Study by the United Nations and World Health Organization*. New York: United Nations.

United Nations (U.N.). 1984. "Mortality and health Policy: Main Issues for the 1980s." Pp. 40-61 in *Population Bulletin of the United Nations*, Number 16 (1984). New York: United Nations Department of International Economic and Social Affairs.

United Nations (U.N.). 1985. *World Population Trends, Population and Development Interrelationships and Population Policies: 1983 Monitoring Report*, Vol. 1. New York: United Nations Department of International Economic and Social Affairs.

United Nations (U.N.). 1986a. "I. Mortality Structure in Five Countries--An Overview." Pp. 1-4 in *Determinants of Mortality Change and Differentials in Developing Countries: The Five Country Case Study Project, Population Studies*, Number 94. New York: United Nations Department of International Economic and Social Affairs.

United Nations (U.N.). 1986b. *World Population Prospects: Estimates and Projections as Assessed in 1984, Population Studies*, Number 98. New York: United Nations Department of International Economic and Social Affairs.

United Nations (U.N.). 1988. *World Population Trends and Policies: 1987 Monitoring Report, Population Studies*, Number 103. New York: United Nations Department of International Economic and Social Affairs.

United Nations (U.N.). 1989. *World Population Prospects 1988, Population Studies*, Number 106. New York: United Nations Department of International Economic and Social Affairs.

United Nations (U.N.D.Y.). 1951, 1954, 1957, 1961, 1967, 1974. *Demographic Yearbook*. New York: United Nations.

United Nations (U.N.S.Y.). 1949-1950, 1951, 1967. *Statistical Yearbook*. New York: United Nations.

United Nations and World Health Organization (U.N. and W.H.O.). 1979. *Proceedings of the Meeting on Socioeconomic Determinants and Consequences of Mortality*, El Colegio de Mexico, Mexico City, 19-25 June 1979. New York and Geneva: United Nations and World Health Organization.

United Nations Secretariat and World Health Organization (U.N. and W.H.O.). 1981. "United Nations/World Health Organization Meeting on Socio-Economic Determinants and Consequences of Mortality, Mexico City, 19-25 June 1979." Pp. 60-74 in *Population Bulletin of the United Nations*, Number 13 (1980). New York: United Nations Department of International Economic and Social Affairs.

Vallin, Jacques. 1981. "Socio-Economic Determinants of Mortality in Industrialized Countries." Pp. 26-41 in *Population Bulletin of the United Nations* Number 13 (1980). New York: United Nations Department of International Economic and Social Affairs.

Vallin, Jacques and Alan Lopez. 1985. "Introduction." Pp. 3-9 in *Health Policy, Social Policy and Mortality Prospects* edited by Jacques Vallin and Alan D. Lopez. Liége, Belgium: Ordina Editions (I.N.E.D. and I.U.S.S.P.).

Vincent, George E. 1927. *The Rockefeller Foundation: A Review for 1926.* New York: Rockefeller Foundation.

Weber, Max. 1946. "Class, Status, and Party." Pp. 180-95 in *Essays in Sociology*, by Max Weber. Oxford: Oxford University Press.

World Health Organization (W.H.O.). 1950-1976. *Official Records*, "Financial Report." Geneva: World Health Organization.

World Health Organization (W.H.O.). 1950-1979. *World Health Statistics Annual*. Geneva: World Health Organization.

Yanagishita, Machiko and Jack M. Guralnik. 1988. "Changing Mortality Patterns That Led Life Expectancy in Japan to Surpass Sweden's: 1972-1982." *Demography* 25: 611-24.

Yang, Shu-O W. Yang and Brian F. Pendleton. 1980. "Socioeconomic Development and Mortality Levels in Less Developed Countries." *Social Biology* 27: 220-29.